PYTHON 3

Python Starter Guide

From Novice to Coder

Laurence Lars Svekis
Sebastian Svekis

Table of Contents

3

Introduction to Python Code for Beginners

Python is a powerful and beginner-friendly programming language that has gained popularity for its simplicity and versatility. This guide will provide you with a gentle introduction to Python code, making it accessible for newcomers to programming.

Python is a popular programming language known for its simplicity and versatility. It is a great choice for beginners because of its easy-to-read syntax and extensive libraries. Here's a summary of how Python code works for beginners:

Basics of Python Quick Overview

Installation: To get started with Python, you need to install it on your computer. You can download the latest version of Python from the official website (python.org) and follow the installation instructions.

Writing Code: Python code is typically written in text files with a ".py" extension. You can use a simple text editor like Notepad or an integrated development environment (IDE) like PyCharm or Visual Studio Code to write Python code.

```
print("Hello, World!")
```

This simple program uses the print() function to display text. Python is known for its straightforward syntax, where you don't need to write complex boilerplate code.

Hello World: Let's start with a classic tradition in programming – printing "Hello, World!" to the screen. Open a Python editor or IDE (Integrated Development Environment). The classic beginner's program is to print "Hello, World!" to the screen. Here's the Python code for it:

```
print("Hello, World!")
```

In Python, print() is used to display text or variables on the screen.

Comments: You can add comments to your code using the # symbol. Comments are ignored by Python but are helpful for explaining your code to yourself and others. For example:

```
# This is a comment
print("Hello, World!")  # This is also a comment
```

Variables: In Python, you can store and manipulate data using variables. You don't have to declare variable types explicitly; Python infers them.
In this code, we've assigned a name (a string) and age (an integer) to variables and then printed their values. Variables are used to store data. Python is dynamically typed, so you don't need to declare a variable's type explicitly. Here's how you create and use variables:

```
name = "Alice"
age = 30
```

```
print(name)
print(age)
```

Data Types: Python supports various data types, including integers, floats, strings, lists, tuples, dictionaries, and more. You can perform operations and manipulations on these data types.

Control Structures: Python uses indentation (whitespace) to define code blocks, like loops and conditionals. Here's an example of a for loop:

```
for i in range(5):
    print(i)
```

This code will print numbers from 0 to 4.

Functions: You can define your own functions in Python. Functions are blocks of reusable code. Here's a simple function:

```
def greet(name):
    print("Hello, " + name + "!")
```

You can call this function with greet("Bob"), and it will print "Hello, Bob!".

Libraries: Python has a vast standard library and numerous third-party libraries that you can use to extend its functionality. You can import libraries using the import statement.

Error Handling: Python provides mechanisms to handle errors gracefully using try and except blocks.

Execution: To run a Python script, you typically save it with a ".py" extension and execute it from the command line using the python command followed by the script's filename.

Debugging: Python IDEs and code editors often come with debugging tools to help you find and fix issues in your code.

Getting Help and Documentation: Python has excellent documentation available online, including the official Python documentation and various tutorials and guides.
Python has an extensive standard library and community-contributed packages. You can access documentation and help within Python:

```
help(print)
```

This will provide information about the print() function.

Python's versatility and user-friendly syntax make it an ideal choice for beginners. As you progress, you can explore more advanced topics such as object-oriented programming, file handling, and web development. Practice, experimentation, and learning from examples are essential for mastering Python programming.

Python is a versatile language used in various domains such as web development, data science, machine learning, and more. As a beginner, you can start by mastering the basics and gradually explore more advanced topics as you become more comfortable with the language. Practice and experimentation are key to becoming proficient in Python programming.

About this Book

"Python Starter Guide: From Novice to Coder" is a comprehensive and hands-on book designed to take beginners on a journey from novice programmers to proficient coders in Python. The book is divided into six chapters, each focusing on a crucial aspect of Python programming.

In Chapter 1, readers are introduced to Python, its importance, and how to set up their development environment. They learn the basics of writing and running Python code, exploring variables, data types, and coding best practices.

Chapter 2 delves deeper into Python coding, covering topics like creating and running Python files, understanding indentation and variable naming rules, and using comments for code clarity. The chapter includes practical exercises to reinforce coding skills.

Chapter 3 explores Python logic and control structures, including conditions, logic, and if...else statements. Readers learn to build interactive applications, use loops for efficient coding, and create reusable Python functions.

Chapter 4 focuses on Python's data structures, including lists, tuples, dictionaries, and sets. Object-oriented programming concepts are introduced, along with custom methods and class inheritance.

Chapter 5 teaches readers how to harness the power of Python modules, including built-in methods and creating custom modules. The chapter covers importing and using various Python modules for different tasks, with hands-on exercises.

Chapter 6 takes Python knowledge to the next level with practical projects and real-world applications. Topics include file handling, project creation (e.g., story-making, games, and data manipulation), working with JSON data, and developing a Python portfolio.

"Python Starter Guide: From Novice to Coder" is ideal for beginners with no prior coding experience. It offers a structured approach to learning Python, complete with practical exercises and real-world examples. The book empowers readers to build coding proficiency and confidence, making it suitable for anyone looking to start their Python programming journey or solidify their coding skills.

Chapter 1 Getting Started with Python

This is for all students who aspire to be a coder in the future and start building smart python apps while reading this book. No previous Python coding experience is required as long as you have a desktop or a laptop to practice the projects.

Introduction to coding with Python designed for students. Equipped with several Python projects and loaded with code examples, you will travel through every essential element of programming and understand how the entire programming of python really works.

Writing code can help with automation and create interactive content dynamically. Once you've learned how to write Python code you will be able to apply it to interact with and perform many useful things.

Getting Started with Coding Python

The objective of this chapter is to guide readers through the process of setting up their developer environment for writing Python code. The chapter starts with instructions on how to install the Python 3 interpreter and how to try out Python code in the terminal. Python 3 had become the recommended and widely adopted version of Python. However, it's important to check the latest developments and recommendations from the Python community, as the programming language continues to evolve.

The chapter then introduces readers to creating simple Python functions in the interpreter and provides guidance on setting up their machine to write Python code. The author covers simple command prompt commands for both Mac and Windows operating systems.

Next, readers learn how to create Python files to save and run their code. The chapter covers variables and how to store values in them, as well as rules for variable naming and commenting in Python code. Readers are provided with exercises to practice adding the values of two variables together and getting the data type of a variable.

The author also introduces the concept of variables that can hold multiple values and casting to set a data type of a value. Readers are given an exercise to create a simple calculator that accepts user input.

In conclusion, the chapter provides key terms and points to remember, and reinforces the importance of setting up a proper environment for writing Python code. Overall, this chapter serves as a practical guide for beginners to get started with writing Python code and provides the foundation for more advanced topics in future chapters.

Why Python and what it is.

Python is an excellent programming language to start with, even if you have never written code before. Programming is about logic and being able to set up steps to accomplish a goal, you don't have to be a math genius or be very technical. Programming is creative, where you plan an approach to a problem and devise the steps to provide the solution. All applications start addressing a problem and providing a solution to solve it.

You can download Python for free, as well many of the best tools to write the code are also free. All you need is a computer and your imagination. There is a lot of support online for Python as many developers are involved in creating Python code. You will find tutorials and code snippets and much more with simple searches on these topics for Python code.

How to Setup your developer environment

Python is perfect for both small and large-scale projects. Designed to help programmers write clear and logical code made to be human-readable. Whitespace and indentations are used to separate blocks of code. Python code when written is easy to read because of the use of indentation and the elegant syntax of the code itself.

Common uses for Python include task automation, data analysis, visualization, and developing web applications. Due to the ease of getting started with Python, it also gets commonly adopted by many non-programmers to help with tasks. One of the most popular programming languages. With a small learning curve, you can get started with Python quickly. Powerful and straightforward. So many people are learning Python, doing cool things and you can get started with Python quickly.

Install the Python 3 Interpreter

The interpreter is the program that reads Python and carries out the instructions from the code. You will need it installed on your computer so that the computer can understand the code.

Python code runs using an interpreter, and there are two major versions of Python. Python version 2 is backward compatible to previous versions. In 2008 Python 3 came along, the codebase was overhauled and updated. Which meant that version 3 was no longer compatible with earlier versions of Python. Package libraries written in 2 are not compatible with Python 3.

Start by downloading Python from the official website at https://python.org. Install the Python 3 interpreter on your computer, which will be needed to read Python applications. You will need this on your computer before you can run Python files, without it the code will not run.

On the Python website select the version of Python for your system.

Files

Version	Operating System
Gzipped source tarball	Source release
XZ compressed source tarball	Source release
macOS 64-bit universal2 installer	macOS
Windows embeddable package (32-bit)	Windows
Windows embeddable package (64-bit)	Windows
Windows embeddable package (ARM64)	Windows
Windows installer (32 -bit)	Windows
Windows installer (64-bit)	Windows
Windows installer (ARM64)	Windows

Figure: Example of files on the Python website

Figure: Go through the steps of installing Python on your computer.

Please note that Mac and Linux computers may come with a version of Python already installed, this is likely Python 2 and you should update to Python 3. Python 2 and Python 3 are intentionally not fully compatible. If you have both versions of Python installed, you can start either interpreter by entering python or python3.

Once you have installed Python or if you want to check to see if Python is installed, open the computer terminal and type python or python3. This will return the version of Python installed on your computer. This is also a way to check that your computer is ready to read and run Python code.

On Windows open the command prompt. Windows might also ask you to install Python when you attempt to open the Python Shell interpreter.

On a Mac to open a terminal with CMD+Spacebar for the spotlight then type Terminal.

Figure: Example of spotlight on a Mac typing terminal.

Type python in the terminal and it will return the version of Python being used, which in the example below is Python 2.7
*Since my Mac already has Python 2 which is the default for python I see a warning message.

Typing python will start the Python interpreter which is indicated by the >>>. From here you can type Python code.

Figure: Python Interpreter in Terminal

The Python interpreter can handle math, try 5 + 5 in the interpreter. It will respond with the evaluated result of the code, which is 10. The response is output on the following line in the terminal.

```
>>> 5 + 5
10
>>>
```

Figure: Python Interpreter calculation

To exit the Python interpreter type quit() with the rounded brackets. This will exit the Python interpreter.

```
>>> quit()
dev@LSvekiss-iMac ~ %
```

Figure: Exit the Python Interpreter back to command prompt

To open the Python3 interpreter, type python3. This will open the interpreter and display the version of the release installed on the computer.

```
dev@LSvekiss-iMac ~ % python3
Python 3.9.6 (default, May  7 2023, 23:32:45)
[Clang 14.0.3 (clang-1403.0.22.14.1)] on darwin
Type "help", "copyright", "credits" or "license" for more information.
>>>
```

Figure: Python3 Open Interpreter

Try the code in the terminal write Python

Exercise output a string value and assign a value to a variable:
Once you are in the Python interpreter type the code
```
print('Hello')
```

Next type
```
name = 'Laurence Svekis'
print(name)
```

You should see a result as in the example below. Don't forget the quotes.

```
>>> print('Hello')
Hello
>>> name = 'Laurence Svekis'
>>> print(name)
Laurence Svekis
>>>
```

Figure: Python3 Open Interpreter statement output

To see more help options type help() in the python interpreter. To exit the help utility type quit. help> quit

```
>>> help()

Welcome to Python 3.9's help utility!
```

Figure: Python help Utility

To exit the interpreter type either quit() or exit() and this will bring you back to the terminal command prompt exiting the Python shell interpreter.

Congratulations you've written your first Python code. Creating output with the print() and assigning a value to a variable name.
Now try functions, which we will cover in much more detail later in the lessons. The function allows you to run a block of code and provide values into the function that can be used in the function.

Exercise Create a simple Python Function in the interpreter.

Open in the Python interpreter. To create a function use the keyword def and create a function name. In this example, we use mes(). The val variable that is nested within the parentheses can hold values and is an argument that can change. Indent the second line and add the print() with the string value of 'Hi' and comma separate the value of the argument referencing it by its variable name val.

```
>>> def mes(val) :
...      print('Hi',val)
...
>>> mes('Laurence')
Hi Laurence
>>> mes('Sebastian')
Hi Sebastian
>>> mes('Jane')
Hi Jane
>>>
```

Figure: Python code

Now you can type mes() adding a string argument within the parenthesis. The value you add in the function parameter will be assigned to val and then can be used within the function. Try different names in mes() and view the results.

Congratulations you have access to Python and have written your first Python code. Once your computer is set up to run Python you can now start creating files that will be used to store the code. Within the Python interpreter, the code will run but you have to retype it each time. This is why we create files.

Introduction to setting up your machine to write Python Code

- Download and install Python3 latest version from https://www.python.org/downloads/
- Download and install code editor https://code.visualstudio.com/

Simple Command Prompt Commands on a MAC
- pwd shows current directory path
- cd changes to a directory within the current folder
- ls lists all files within the current directory
- cs ../ moves down one level from the current directory

```
webs-iMac:~ web$ pwd
/Users/web
webs-iMac:~ web$ cd sites
webs-iMac:sites web$ ls
JS                PYTHON
JavaScript        app
OLDFiles          book2.html
Old Apps          db.json
webs-iMac:sites web$ pwd
/Users/web/sites
webs-iMac:sites web$ cd ../
webs-iMac:~ web$ pwd
/Users/web
webs-iMac:~ web$
```

Figure: Directory listing using command line

Windows OS install and Setup of Python

- open search and type command prompt
- Once the terminal is open type python --version which will show the default python install typically Version 2
- Type python3 --version which will show the version of Python 3 installed
- Type python3 to open shell interpreter for Python code
- Type 5+10 and note the result

- to exit the shell interpreter type either quit() or exit() this will bring you back to the terminal command prompt

- type help() to open the Python help utility`

Simple Command Prompt Commands on a Windows PC

- cd changes to a directory within the current folder

- dir lists all files within the current directory

- cs ../ moves down one level from the current directory

```
C:\Users\web>dir
 Volume in drive C has no label.
 Volume Serial Number is 0A0D-6E27

 Directory of C:\Users\web

2021-09-22  02:55 PM    <DIR>          .
2021-09-22  02:55 PM    <DIR>          ..
2021-09-22  02:55 PM    <DIR>          3D Objects
2021-09-22  02:55 PM    <DIR>          Contacts
2019-12-07  04:14 AM    <DIR>          Desktop
2021-09-22  02:54 PM    <DIR>          Documents
```

Figure: Terminal Directory navigation

Create Python files Run the code and save

You will also need an editor to write the code and a terminal to run the code. The editor that I will be using within this course is Visual Studio Code https://code.visualstudio.com/ It comes with a built-in terminal so that you can write the code and also run the code in the same application. There are many alternatives to using Visual Studio Code, one commonly used IDE is PyCharm https://www.jetbrains.com/pycharm/

Once the editor is installed, open it. The best practice is to install the Python Extension which will help transform the editor into a Python IDE. IDE is short for an integrated development environment which is how we refer to a software application that facilitates the writing of code used by programmers for software development.

Install your editor and open the editor to create a new file.
In Visual Studio Code select to install the Python Extension.

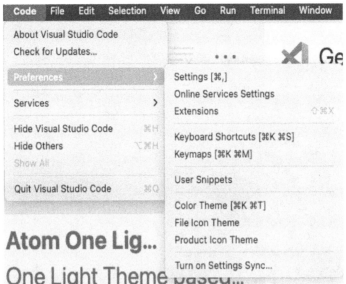

Figure: Using Visual Studio Code to select Preferences menu

The Python extension for Visual Studio Code is named Python. It can be searched for within the extensions. Once selected, install it into the IDE and you will be ready to write Python code in Visual Studio Code IDE.

Python extension for Visual Studio Code

Figure: Adding Python Extension to Visual Studio Code

Select to create a new file.

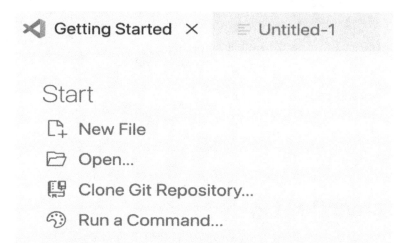

Figure: Start Menu for Visual Studio Code Editor

You can select the language being used for the code, or once you save the file with the py extension it will automatically use the python language. Creating a file in the IDE is like using a text editor to create other types of computer files.

Create a new folder to use as the storage for the Python files you will be creating. This is good practice as it will make them easier to find. Within the editor, you can also create workspaces that can be used to group project files together that are from related work making them easier to find.

≡ Untitled-1 ✕

1 |Select a language to get started.

Figure: Creating a new file in Visual Studio Code

Create the file and save the file using the py extension.

 test1.py   ✕

   1

Figure: New file in Code editor named test1.py

When creating files on your computer you would need to provide the file type, which is in the name of the file at the end. The file extension can be found at the end of the file name and is added by separating the actual file name and the extension by a period. To create a Python file you would use the extension .py;

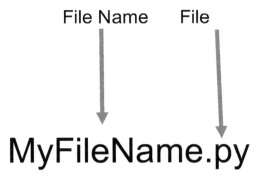

Figure: Example of naming a file and adding it as a Python file with the py extension.

Create a new file and give it a name, add the py extension to indicate to your computer what applications can be used to open the file type. Give the file a name with the extension py. For example, you can open the editor and save the file as test1.py Also open the terminal either in your editor or as the second application.

To open the terminal in Visual Studio code, you can select from the top menu or use the keyboard shortcut.

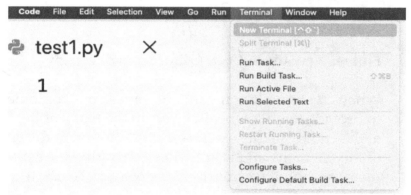

Figure: Code editor opening terminal from top menu bar

The terminal will open at the bottom of the editor. This will default to the same folder directory as the file you have opened, which is convenient so you can easily run the file.

Figure: Example of terminal opened at the bottom of the code editor

Getting Started creating your first Python File

Walk through the first steps to set up your computer to be ready to write Python code. How to install Python on a Mac and Windows Machine. How to set up and prepare your code editor for writing Python Code. Save the file as filename.py

To run the python file you can type python filename.py also, to run in python3 you suffix the word python with 3 python3 filename.py

Within the Python file add the line of code print() and within the parenthesis create a string value. The String value is represented by characters that have quotes around them. They can be either single or double quotes.

```
print('Hello World')
```

```
🐍 test1.py    ✕
  1    print('Hello World')
  2
```

PROBLEMS   OUTPUT   TERMINAL   DEBUG CONSOLE

```
webs-iMac:Python web$ python3 test1.py
Hello World
```

Figure: Terminal Directory navigation

In the same file add a new line of code. Type the print()
and this time include a math statement adding a set of
values together. The numbers can be any number.
The code will return the response with the total of the
values.

```
print('Hello World')
print(5+10+15)
```

In the terminal select the file and run the code with the
python3 prefix to the file name.

```
test1.py        ×
1       print('Hello World')
2       print(5+10+15)

PROBLEMS    OUTPUT    TERMINAL    DEBUG CONSOLE

webs-iMac:Python web$ python3 test1.py
Hello World
webs-iMac:Python web$ python3 test1.py
Hello World
30
```

Figure: Terminal Directory navigation

Variables storing values.

Create a variable that can be used to hold a value. You
can assign values to variables using the = equal sign.
Then using print() add the variable as the argument
within the print() parenthesis.

```
print('Hello World')
print(5+10+15)
```

```
message = 'Hello World'
print(message)
```

Run the file again and check the results.

```
test1.py    ×
1    print('Hello World')
2    print(5+10+15)
3    message = 'Hello World'|
4    print(message)
```

PROBLEMS   OUTPUT   TERMINAL   DEBUG CONSOLE

```
webs-iMac:Python web$ python3 test1.py
Hello World
30
Hello World
webs-iMac:Python web$ []
```

Figure: Executing a Python File

Python uses indentation and how it works is that the indentation indicates a block of code. In Python indentation is very important.

Indentation of Python Code

Indentation refers to the spacing at the beginning of the line of code. This is an extra whitespace that is added. In Python this is important as it not only makes the code more readable but also unlike other programming languages Python uses the indentation to indicate blocks of code.

Blocks of code are separate chunks of related code that are expected to be run together. It is separated from the rest of the code within blocks. This helps identify the code that needs to be run.

When using conditions, the indentation represents the code that will be run if the condition is true.

```
if 10 < 20:
    print('That works 10 is less than 20')
    print('this too')
print('outside the block will run
anyway')
```

Result:
That works 10 is less than 20
this too
outside the block will run anyway

```
if 30 < 20:
    print('That works 30 is less than 20')
    print('this too')
print('outside the block will run
anyway')
```

Result:
outside the block will run anyway

Without the indentation the code will run all the lines that are not indented and would have no way of knowing which block is intended to be executed only if the condition is true.

One of the most important concepts of programming. Variables are at the core of programming. They are containers that can hold information, which can then be easily referenced within the code and returned when needed. Think of a variable to reference something that might change, like a box where you can put items into it and return back the contents of that box by selecting the box label.

- Strings can be single or double quote.

- Variable names are case-sensitive which means that val is not the same as Val or vAl or vaL. These would all be different variables.

Rules for variable naming:

1. Must start with letter or _ underscore.

2. Can use a-zA-Z0-9_ alphanumeric characters within the variable name.

3. Case sensitive

4. Use Camel case to indicate words in the variable name.

5. Can only be one word no spaces.

When naming variables, you can use camel case or underscores for multiple word variable names. This will make them more readable. When the words are separated by the underscore it's also referred to as snake case.

Consider the variable myfullname which can be created as myFullName
or my_full_name , both will work and make it more readable.   It's important to be consistent when naming. Use your best judgment when creating names, try to make them meaningful for the content that will be assigned to the variables.

Add new statements into the code that assign values of the numbers to letters, a,b,c
Then assign to a new variable named total all a+b+c
Using print() output the response values into the terminal.

You can also assign the same value to all variable names using the = sign

```
print('Hello World')
print(5+10+15)
message = 'Hello World'
print(message)
a = 5
b = 10
c = 15
total = a + b + c
print(a+b+c)
print(total)
```

```
test1.py  ×
1    print('Hello World')
2    print(5+10+15)
3    message = 'Hello World'
4    print(message)
5    a = 5
6    b = 10
7    c = 15
8    total = a + b + c
9    print(a+b+c)
10   print(total)


PROBLEMS    OUTPUT    TERMINAL    DEBUG CONSOLE


webs-iMac:Python web$ python3 test1.py
Hello World
30
Hello World
30
30
webs-iMac:Python web$ []
```

Figure: Code and output result within Code Editor Terminal

Commenting in Python Code

Comments can explain code, making it more readable and great for testing when you want lines of code not to execute. You can also provide information that can be used later and referred to later by yourself or other developers.

Use comments to block out a few lines of code so that they do not run. Also, add comments at the end of the line of code to provide more details about what the expected result is and the reason for the line of code.

```
#print('Hello World')
#print(5+10+15)
message = 'Hello World'
```

```
print(message)
a = 5
b = 10
c = 15
total = a + b + c #adding the values
print(a+b+c)
print(total) #printing the total value
```

You can also block out multiple lines of code using triple quotes.

Try out the commenting multiple lines. These can be used while debugging or as a way to add information to the file.

```
#print('Hello World')
#print(5+10+15)
message = 'Hello World'
print(message)
"""
a = 5
b = 10
c = 15
total = a + b + c #adding the values
print(a+b+c)
"""
total = 'unknown'
print(total) #printing the total value
```

We've provided examples of two types of variables, strings with a set of characters contained within the quotes. Numbers that were numeric values that are written without quotes.

Exercise adding the values of 2 variables together.

1. create a value of your first name and assign it to a variable named first
2. Create a value for you last name and assign it to a variable named last
3. create a new variable named fullName and assign the value of both first and last as the value for this variable.
4. Using print output the fullName result into the terminal
5. Fix the issue with the missing spacing.

```
first = 'Laurence'
last = 'Svekis'
fullName = first + last
print(fullName)
```

Result:
LaurenceSvekis

Fixed spacing challenge code

```
first = 'Laurence'
last = 'Svekis'
space = ' '
fullName = first + space + last
print(fullName)
```

To find out the data type you can use a method called type(). Just like the print method it accepts an argument which then gets used to return a response. In the case of type() it will respond with the type of variable that is requested.

Exercise to get the variable data type

1. create a variable with a string, and a second one that has a number assigned to it. Using print output the type() with the variable contained in the rounded brackets.

2. Create a variable and assign the type() of the first variable to it.

3. The output that results in the terminal with print()

```
user = 'Laurence'
val = 100
print(type(user))
print(type(val))
t1 = type(user)
print(t1)
```

Terminal Result:
<class 'str'>
<class 'int'>
<class 'str'>

You can assign multiple values in variables by comma separation of variable names and assigning to comma-separated values. Comma separate for multiple variables in one line.

You can also reassign a new value to a variable with the equal sign.

Assigning different data types to a variable will change the data type of that variable.

To assign the same value to multiple variables you can use an equal sign between them.

```
a,b,c = 5,10,15
print(a+b+c)
user = 'Laurence'
user = 'Svekis'
print(user)
user = 5
print(user)
d = e = f = 100
print(d+e+f)
```

Terminal Result:
30
Svekis
5
300

Variables that can hold multiple values.

Using a collection, you can assign those values to a number of variables within one statement.

To access the content contained within the collection you can use its index value. Index values start at zero which means that the first item in the collection will have an index of zero.

```
data = ['Laurence','Svekis',100]
print(data[0])
print(data[1])
print(data[2])
```

terminal result:
Laurence
Svekis
100

You can also assign the data from the collection to separate variables, as this collection has 3 items within it, you can use 3 variables names to assign the values to.

```
first,last,vid = data
print(first + ' ' + last )
```

result:
Laurence Svekis

If you try to add the number data type to the string it will throw an error. You need to convert the value of the number into a string to be able to output it within the same concatenate string value. The error that will be thrown when the different types are concatenated will be TypeError: can only concatenate str (not "int") to str.

To convert the number to a string you can use the str() method.

```
data = ['Laurence','Svekis',100]
first,last,vid = data
vid = str(vid)
print(first + ' ' + last + ' ID:' + vid)
```

Result:
Laurence Svekis ID:100

Another data type that is commonly used is the boolean value. This is great for logic. Boolean can be either True or False - must be capitalized.

```
a = True
print(type(a))
b = False
print(type(b))
c = 5 > 10
print(c)
print(type(c))
```

Result:

<class 'bool'>

<class 'bool'>
False
<class 'bool'>

Casting to set a data type of a value.

If you want to set the data type of the variable, you can
set it with casting methods. Include the value that you
want to convert into the specific data type using the
methods str() for strings int() for integers or float() for
float values.

```
a = 100
print(type(a))
a= str(a)
print(type(a))
a = int(a)
print(type(a))
a= float(a)
print(type(a))
print(a)
```

Result
<class 'int'>
<class 'str'>
<class 'int'>
<class 'float'>
100.0

How to get User Input for interaction with your Python Code

Within your code, you can request the user provide input. The input will be a string data type by default. You can assign the response of the user input to a variable that can be used within your code.

```python
print('What is your name?')
userName = input()
print('welcome to Python, '+userName)
```

Result
what is your name?
Laurence
welcome to Python, Laurence

The string value of the question can also be added as the argument value within the input to shorten the above code.

```python
userName = input('what is your name?')
print('welcome to Python, '+userName)
```

The input response value is a string. If you want to add to the value and expect the result to be an integer you can use the int() to convert it. The below example will throw an error since you cannot concatenate the str to an int.

```python
question = 'How old are you?'
age = input(question)
```

```
print('Your age is '+ age)
plus5 = age + 5
```

To fix the above code use the cast. You will need to convert it to an integer to add it to another integer and then convert it back to a string to join it to the rest of the string output message.

```
question = 'How old are you?'
age = input(question)
print('Your age is '+ age)
ageI = int(age)
plus5 = ageI+5
print('In 5 years you will be '+str(plus5))
```

result
How old are you?
Your age is 6
In 5 years you will be 11

Exercise Create a simple Calculator.

Using the input, ask the user for two numbers, take the numbers and convert them to integers so that you can add them together. Create an output message to the user with the total and the equation for the two numbers added together.

Exercise:
1. Use the input to ask the user for a first number and then a second input for the second number.

2. These values need to be integers so that they can be added together. Convert them to integers and add them together. Create a variable for the total.

3. Create a string that can provide the message of the values and what the calculation is of the numbers. Convert the integers back to strings with str()

4. Print the calculation into the terminal.

5. Print the total with a message to the user.

```
num1 = int(input("First Number : "))
num2 = int(input("Second Number : "))
total = num1 + num2
cal = str(num1) + "+" + str(num2) + "=" +
str(total)
message = "Your Total is " + str(total)
print(cal)
print(message)
```

Result
First Number : 6
Second Number : 12
6+12=18
Your Total is 18

Conclusion

Congratulations, good job, you are now set and, on your way, to write can learn more about coding with Python. Now that you have set up your computer to write Python code you can jump right in anytime to try coding. Use the code being presented and try it, also try combining code to see what happens. The best way to learn is to try the code out for yourself!

Getting setup to write Python code is important, as once you are properly set up you can then open and write code. Whichever editor you choose ensures you can create python files and run the files in a terminal. Try creating a few Python files and run some of the code examples from this lesson to be ready to move on to the upcoming lessons which are going to focus on coding in Python.

Key Terms/Points to remember.
- Create folders to hold new projects.

- Create well named files so that when you reference them and open them later it will be quicker to find them.

- Practice writing statements in both the python shell in the terminal directly as well as creating python files.

- Try variations and combinations of the code being presented to see what happens.

Chapter 2 Get Coding Python

Within this chapter we will be covering the basics of coding Python. By the end of the chapter you should be able to create your own scripts and run them. Strings and string methods will be covered, string methods provide additional functionality that can be done with string values. Conditions in code allow for applying of logic, they are Boolean in nature. Looping code saves time when blocks of code need to be run multiple times. Functions within Python provide a way to run blocks of code, calling prebuilt blocks allows better control over when certain actions happen. Variables are set within blocks of code, and they cannot be accessed on outside blocks. The global keyword can be used to control the variables values and where they are being referenced from.

There are several exercises in this chapter to help practice and learn more about the topics covered. There is a favorite number game, where the objective is to demonstrate how to apply logic to inputs. The last exercise is also a number guessing game, where the objective is to apply the code covered in the chapter to create an interactive mini game. The application will guide the player through the steps of the gameplay, providing feedback and continuing the gameplay until the solution is found.

Exercise: Create a file run the code as interactive

This exercise will provide an opportunity to create a simple file that can be run to see the output in the terminal. Open the editor and try some code in this lesson.

1. You can use File > New File to open and create a new file.
2. Create and save the file into a main directory that you will use for the lessons of this course.
3. Create a folder to store all the files within, so that they will be easier to find.
4. Once you've created the file, save it with an extension of .py
5. Within the file use print('Laurence Svekis') with you name in the quotes

The below image provides an example of what the exercise achieves, you can change the output name to your own as you customize it.

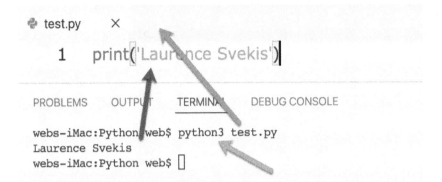

Figure: Python code and output

Open the terminal and type the python3 and then the file name. At the cursor type python3 then the name of the file. This will run the code in the file, which prints the name out into the terminal.

This line is what is known as shebang. #!/usr/bin/env python3

Include the shebang line at the top of the script file, which will help the machine or anyone who views the file to determine the environment to run the file in. The shebang line helps make your program executable so that the program can be installed like other applications on your computer.

To make your file executable without having to write python3 before executing the file, run the below in your terminal. This will set the file attribute to be executable. chmod +x filename.py

After this is set you can then execute your file by typing its filename, the file itself will provide what type of code it is, as well the file itself will be then executable.

```
1    #!/usr/bin/env python3
2    print('Laurence Svekis')
```

PROBLEMS   OUTPUT   TERMINAL   DEBUG CONSOLE

```
webs-iMac:Python web$ chmod +x test.py
webs-iMac:Python web$ ./test.py
Laurence Svekis
```

Figure: Python Terminal set up

Adding the shebang at the top of your file will tell the machine that is running the code which environment to run it in. You can also type the env python3 to open into the python3 environment directly from the terminal.

```
#!/usr/bin/env python3
print('Laurence Svekis')
```

To check the data type use the type method with the variable nested between the rounded brackets.

```
user = 'Laurence Svekis'
print(user)
print(type(user))
```

Output result will be

```
Laurence Svekis
<class 'str'>
```

Strings and String Methods

You can also return parts of the string back using the index value, indexing starts at 0. To return the first character in the string use the [0] in the below example this will be L, to return the sixth character use the [5] in the below example the result will be n.

```
user = 'Laurence Svekis'
print(user[0])#L
print(user[5]) #n
```

You can also use the negative, which will start from the end of the string and go backwards. This is also a way to slice a part of a string using the : before the index number to return characters up until that value, or after to return characters after.

```
user = 'Laurence Svekis'
print(user[-5]) #v
print(user[:8]) #Laurence
print(user[9:]) #Svekis
```

Exercise : How to select parts of a string value

A simple example of how to return parts of a string value, using various starting indexes.

1. Set up you name as the variable value for user.

2. Using the slicing return your first name and set it as the value of first.

3. Using the slicing return your last name and set it as the value of last.

4. Set the space as a variable named space.

5. Print the results of your first and last name using the variables.

```
user = 'Laurence Svekis'
first = user[:8]
last = user[9:]
space = user[8]
print(first + space + last)
```

Result will output: Laurence Svekis

String methods allow you to make updates to the string characters, such as transform them to upper- or lower-case characters. There is also a way to capitalize the string.

Select a string and join the upper() to change the letters all to uppercase characters, or lower() to change the letters all to lowercase letters. You can also use capitalize() to change the string contents to capitalized.

```
str1 = 'welCOME to the WeBSIte'
val1 = str1.upper()
print(val1)
print(str1.lower())
print(str1.capitalize())
```

```
WELCOME  TO  THE  WEBSITE
welcome  to  the  website
Welcome  to  the  website
```
Figure: Output of the results of the code

Exercise: how to use String methods

Converting strings with methods that return the updated value of the string.

1. Use the code from the previous exercise and upper case your first name
2. Lower case you last name
3. Join the first and last name together and capitalize them.

```
user = 'Laurence Svekis'
first = user[:8].upper()
last = user[9:].lower()
space = user[8]
print(first + space + last)
print(len(user))
capme = (first + last).capitalize()
print(capme)
```

This Python code performs various operations on a string stored in the user variable, which is set to the value 'Laurence Svekis'. Here's a step-by-step explanation of the code:

1. user = 'Laurence Svekis': This line initializes the user variable with the string 'Laurence Svekis', which presumably represents a person's name.

2. first = user[:8].upper(): This line extracts the first part of the name, from the beginning of the string up to the 8th character (excluding the character at index 8), using slicing. Then, it converts this extracted substring to uppercase using the .upper() method. The result is stored in the first variable.

3. last = user[9:].lower(): This line extracts the last part of the name, starting from the 9th character to the end of the string, using slicing. Then, it converts this extracted substring to lowercase using the .lower() method. The result is stored in the last variable.

4. space = user[8]: This line extracts the character at index 8 from the user string, which is the space character between the first name and last name. It is stored in the space variable.

5. print(first + space + last): This line concatenates the uppercase first name, the space character, and the

lowercase last name, and then prints the result. This effectively prints the name with the first name in uppercase, a space, and the last name in lowercase.

6. print(len(user)): This line calculates and prints the length of the user string using the len() function. It will output 15, which is the number of characters in the string 'Laurence Svekis'.

7. capme = (first + last).capitalize(): This line first concatenates the first and last names (in their original case) and then capitalizes the entire resulting string using the .capitalize() method. This means that only the first letter of the entire name will be capitalized, while the rest will be in lowercase. The result is stored in the capme variable.

Now, if we consider the original string 'Laurence Svekis', the code will produce the following output:
LAURENCE svekis
15
Laurence svekis

The code demonstrates string manipulation using slicing, uppercase and lowercase conversions, length calculation, and capitalization.

String Functions Python, can update and manipulate the string values with useful built in string methods that can be applied to strings.

To remove surrounding whitespace use the strip() method. The below code has a string value with digits, it will not be numeric with the whitespace around it. To remove the whitespace so that just the digits remain use the strip() method.

```
id = " 555   "
print(id.isnumeric())
nid = id.strip()
print(nid.isnumeric())
```

Using the replace method the values of a string can be replaced with new string characters. The first argument is the value of the character(s) to be replaced, the second is the replacing value.

Turn Laurence Svekis into LaurXncX SvXkis

```
id = " 555   "
print(id.isnumeric())
nid = id.strip()
print(nid.isnumeric())
```

What will the output of the below code produce?

```
name = "    Laurence Svekis    "
val =
name[6:].replace("e","").strip().upper()
print(val)
```

Answer: URNC SVKIS

The in and not in keywords can be used to check if a value exists within a string.

```
name = "Laurence Svekis"
findThis = "Sve"
print((findThis in name))
print((findThis not in name))
```

Exercise: How to clean up a string value with string methods

This exercise is designed to demonstrate how to remove whitespace and reformat a string value.

1. Create a variable with whitespace surrounding you name.
2. Using strip() and split() convert the name into a list of two items first and last name.
3. Using join() join the entries in the list together separated by a dash.
4. Print the results into the terminal.

```
name = "    Laurence Svekis    "
val = name.strip().split(" ")
print(name)
val1 = '-'.join(val)
print(val1)
```

Output :
   Laurence Svekis
Laurence-Svekis

Conditions and Logic If .. Else Statements

Conditions allow us to apply logic into our Python code. Indentation is important as it helps Python understand the block of code that needs to run if the condition is true. A condition runs a Boolean result, which is either True or False. This then can be used to run a block of code depending on the result. Boolean values are capitalized without quotes, writing them as True or False. The code that is run if the condition is true is after the colon:.

Indentation is used to separate out the new block of code from the surrounding code block.

Exercise condition output

The condition example will check if a value of the Boolean is true, if it is True then the result will be the block of code will be run, if its false the block of code will not run.

1. Create a variable named boo and assign a value of True to it
2. Using the condition keyword if output the Boo was true into the terminal if the value of boo is true.
3. Switch the value of boo to the opposite, True or False try both and see what happens.

```
boo = True
if boo: print('Boo was true')
```

To add multiple lines of code that will run, use the indentation. The below example will only output the one line of code 'new line 2'

```
boo = False
if boo:
    print('Boo was true')
    print('new line 1')
print('new line 2')
```

To provide a result if the condition is not true the else keyword can be used. To add multiple lines of code to run on else use the new line, and indentation of the code that will be run. The below will result in the 3 lines of code being output.

Result:
Boo was false.
new line 3
new line 2

```
boo = False
if boo:
    print('Boo was true')
    print('new line 1')
else:
    print('Boo was false')
    print('new line 3')
print('new line 2')
```

To check on a second condition use the elif with the condition, then the same format with the colon and the indentation for the lines of code.

```
val = 1
if val >4:
    print('Great than 4')
elif val < 4:
    print('Less than 4')
else :
    print('must be equal')
```

Shorthand allows you to execute it in one line of code. The below is the same code using 3 conditions written as one statement.

```
print('Great than 4') if val >4 else
print('Less than 4') if val < 4 else
print('must be equal')
```

An operator can be used to check the result of two values, using a condition allows for the addition of logic to the statement.

```
boo = False
a = 500
b = 1500
print(a < b)
if boo: print("boo is True")
```

More lines of code can be added, if it's indented for each condition. It will run each of the independent lines.

```
if a < b:
  a = 1000
  print(a)
  print("True")
```

```
elif a > b:
  print("a is greater")
else:
  print("a and b must be the same equal")
```

The statements can be written on a single line, depending on the result of the condition the result will vary.

```
boo = False
a = 500
b = 1500
print("Hello") if boo else print("world")
print("Equal") if a==b else print("B
bigger") if b > a else print("A must be
bigger")
```

String methods can be helpful in checking to see if they can be converted to an integer. You can use a condition to check and run a block of code depending on the Boolean value of a variable. The isnumeric() method returns a Boolean value of True if all the characters in the string value are numeric (0-9), otherwise it will return a value of False. This is a way to check the data type of the input value.

To check if a string value is numeric use the isnumeric() method, which will return a Boolean value of true if it's numeric or false if it's not. This Boolean result can then be used within the condition to ensure a value is numeric and convert the value to a number using the int()

```
a = 5
print(type(a))
b = '5'
```

```
print(type(b))
print(b.isnumeric())
```

This Python code demonstrates the use of variables and the type() function to determine the data type of a variable, as well as the isnumeric() method to check if a string contains only numeric characters. Here's a step-by-step explanation of the code:

1. a = 5: This line assigns the integer value 5 to the variable a. As a result, a is of data type int, which represents integers.

2. print(type(a)): This line uses the type() function to determine the data type of the variable a and prints the result. It will output <class 'int'>, indicating that a is an integer.

3. b = '5': This line assigns the string value '5' to the variable b. As a result, b is of data type str, which represents strings.

4. print(type(b)): This line uses the type() function to determine the data type of the variable b and prints the result. It will output <class 'str'>, indicating that b is a string.

5. print(b.isnumeric()): This line checks whether the string stored in the variable b ('5') consists of only numeric characters using the isnumeric() method. The isnumeric() method returns True if all characters in the string are numeric (digits), and it returns False otherwise.

Here's the expected output of the code:
<class 'int'>
<class 'str'>
True

Explanation of the output:
- The first print statement confirms that a is of data type int.
- The second print statement confirms that b is of data type str.
- The third print statement checks if the string '5' in variable b is numeric, and it prints True because all characters in '5' are numeric digits.

In summary, this code demonstrates how to determine the data type of variables using the type() function and how to check if a string is numeric using the isnumeric() method. It highlights the difference between an integer (int) and a string (str) and shows that you can perform operations specific to each data type.

Favorite Number Checker Mini App

Create a mini application from the content of this section the user their favorite number and then check if its a valid number that can be converted into an integer and used within your code.
1. Create an input to receive the users favorite number
2. Check if the number is numeric, output the Boolean result
3. Create a message that the input is not a number

4. Create a condition that if the number is numeric output the type and update the message to say that the input is numeric.

5. Print the message to the terminal

```
val = input("What is your favorite number
1-9: ")
boo = val.isnumeric()
print(boo)
message = "Sorry not a number "
if(boo):
   num = int(val)
   print(type(num))
   message = "Great your number is " + val
print(message)
```

Second part of this challenge is to simplify the code from the previous challenge. Updated version with less lines of code for the number checker:

1. Using input() ask the users favorite number

2. Check if the value that was input is a number, if it is output that the value is a number.

3. If it's not a number output that the number was not a number.

```
val = input("What is your favorite number
1-9: ")
boo = val.isnumeric()
```

```
if(boo):
   message = "Great your number is " + val
else:
    message = "Sorry not a number "
print(message)
```

This Python code is a program that prompts the user to enter their favorite number, checks if the input is a numeric value, and then provides a response based on the input. It also demonstrates how to convert a valid numeric input into an integer and print its type. Here's a step-by-step explanation of the code:

1. val = input("What is your favorite number 1-9: "): This line prompts the user to enter their favorite number and stores the user's input as a string in the variable val.

2. boo = val.isnumeric(): This line checks whether the val variable contains a numeric value. The isnumeric() method returns True if all characters in the string are numeric (digits), and it returns False otherwise. The result is stored in the boo variable as a boolean value.

3. print(boo): This line prints the boolean value stored in the boo variable, indicating whether the user's input is numeric. It will print either True or False.

4. message = "Sorry not a number ": This line initializes the message variable with the string "Sorry not a number," assuming that the input is not numeric. This is the default message.

5. if(boo):: This line begins an if statement that checks the value of boo. If boo is True, indicating that the user's input consists of numeric characters, the program proceeds with the following code block.

6. num = int(val): Inside the if block, this line converts the string stored in the val variable into an integer using the int() function and assigns it to the num variable. This assumes that the input is a valid integer.

7. print(type(num)): This line prints the data type of the num variable using the type() function. It will print something like <class 'int'> to indicate that num is an integer.

8. message = "Great your number is " + val: If the input is numeric, this line creates a message by concatenating the string "Great your number is " with the user's input stored in the val variable. The resulting message is stored in the message variable.

9. print(message): Finally, the program prints the message variable, which contains either "Great your number is [user's input]" if the input is numeric or "Sorry not a number" if the input is not numeric.

Here's an example of how the program works:

- If the user enters "7," the program will print True, the type of num, and "Great your number is 7" because the input is numeric.

- If the user enters "eleven," the program will print False and "Sorry not a number" because the input is not numeric.

   This code demonstrates input validation, type conversion, and conditional statements to handle user input based on whether it is numeric or not.

   This Python code is a simple program that prompts the user to enter their favorite number, checks if the input is a numeric value, and then provides a response based on the input. Here's a step-by-step explanation of the code:

1. val = input("What is your favorite number 1-9: "): This line prompts the user to enter their favorite number and stores the user's input as a string in the variable val.

2. boo = val.isnumeric(): This line checks whether the val variable contains a numeric value. The isnumeric() method returns True if all characters in the string are numeric (digits), and it returns False otherwise. The result is stored in the boo variable as a Boolean value.

3. if(boo):: This line begins an if statement that checks the value of boo. If boo is True, indicating that the user's input consists of numeric characters, the program proceeds with the following code block.

4. message = "Great your number is " + val: If the input is numeric, this line creates a message by concatenating the string "Great your number is " with the user's input stored in the val variable. The resulting message is stored in the message variable.

5. else: If the if condition in step 3 is not met (i.e., if the input is not numeric), the program proceeds to the else block.

6. message = "Sorry not a number ": In the else block, this line sets the message variable to "Sorry not a number," indicating that the user did not enter a numeric value.

7. print(message): Finally, the program prints the message variable, which contains either "Great your number is [user's input]" if the input is numeric or "Sorry not a number" if the input is not numeric.

Here's an example of how the program works:

- If the user enters "7," the program will print "Great your number is 7" because the input is numeric.
- If the user enters "eleven," the program will print "Sorry not a number" because the input is not numeric.
- If the user enters "3.14," the program will also print "Sorry not a number" because the input contains non-numeric characters.

This code demonstrates a simple form of input validation to determine if the user's input is numeric and provides a corresponding message based on the input.

String formatting can add values into a string using the {} brackets. Chain the format() method after the string value, then add the arguments for the values you want to add into the string. The number of arguments should match the number of {} brackets:

```
first = 'Laurence'
last = 'Svekis'
str1 = 'Hello, {} {} great to see
you'.format(first,last)
print(str1)
```

Exercise Bouncer determine if the user is allowed in.

This exercise applies logic to input values coming from the user. Depending on the input value coming from the user, there will be a response. The logic is applied to an age, where depending on the age of the user they will have different types of access allowed.

1. Create an application that will ask the user their age.

2. Depending on the age, first check if the response is a number. If it's not a number, reject them and provide a message back. If it's a number then check to see if the

value is allowed in and can drink which is 21+, if they are 18-20 they can come in but not drink and lastly if they are 17 or less they should not be allowed in.

3. Create the application to follow these rules!

```python
age = input("How old are you? ")
boo = age.isnumeric()
if boo:
   print("Thank you I am checking if you can come in...")
   val = int(age)
   if(val >= 21):
        print("Great you are allowed in and can drink")
   elif(val >= 18):
        print("Come in but can't drink")
   else:
        print("You are not allowed in.  Not old enough")
else:
   print("We need your age!")
```

This Python code is a simple program that takes user input for their age and then determines whether they are old enough to enter a place (presumably a venue or event) and whether they are old enough to consume alcoholic drinks based on their age. Here's a step-by-step explanation of the code:

1. age = input("How old are you? "): This line prompts the user to enter their age and stores the input as a string in the variable age.
2. boo = age.isnumeric(): This line checks if the age variable contains a numeric value (digits only). The isnumeric() method returns True if all characters in the string are numeric, and False otherwise. The result is stored in the boo variable.
3. if boo:: This line checks the value of boo. If it's True, it means that the user entered a numeric age, and the program proceeds with age-related checks.
4. print("Thank you I am checking if you can come in..."): This line is a simple informational message to let the user know that the program is checking their age.
5. val = int(age): It converts the age variable, which is a string, into an integer and stores it in the variable val.
6. if(val >= 21):: This line checks if the value of val (the user's age) is greater than or equal to 21. If it is, the program prints a message indicating that the user is allowed to enter and drink.
7. elif(val >= 18):: If the previous condition is not met, this line checks if the user's age is greater than or equal to 18

but less than 21. If so, the user is allowed to enter but not allowed to drink.

8. else:: If neither of the previous conditions is met, this line is executed, indicating that the user is not old enough to enter.

9. If the initial condition if boo: is False, meaning the user did not enter a numeric age, the program prints "We need your age!" to prompt the user to provide valid input.

Here's a sample execution flow:
- If the user enters "25," they will be allowed in and able to drink.

- If the user enters "19," they will be allowed in but not able to drink.

- If the user enters "16," they will not be allowed in because they are not old enough.

- If the user enters "abc," they will be prompted to enter their age again.

This code is a simple example of input validation and conditional statements in Python to handle user input based on their age.

Looping Code

Python has loop commands that allow you to run the block of code several times. They require a condition that is true and will run the block, a value that will eventually change so the loop can break and stop.

While loop allows us to run blocks of code multiple times. There are options using the keyword continue to skip an iteration as well as using the keyboard break to leave and stop the loop. In addition to the loop there is also an option to provide an alternative output once the loop condition is no longer true and run an else block of code.

To loop a block of code 10 times, create a variable that will hold the starting value. Using the while add the condition to break out of the loop. Print the value of i as it iterates through the loop and increment the value of i plus 1. This can be written as i=i+1 or in shorthand i+=1

```
i = 0
while i < 10:
    print(i)
    i+=1
```

To stop a loop the break statement can be used, this will stop the looping even if the condition is still true. Adding a condition that runs the break code will stop the loop, in the below example the output will stop at 4 as the value of i will be greater than 4 and not output.

```
i = 0
while i < 10:
```

```
print(i)
if i>3:
    break
i=i+1
```

Continue statement can be to skip over a current iteration and move on to the next. Using the % modulus will check to see if a value has a remainder.

To check if a value is even or odd you can use the %2 value.

```
print(6%2) #return 0
print(7%2) #return 1
```

This Python code demonstrates the use of the modulo operator % to calculate the remainder of division between two numbers. Here's an explanation of each line:

1. print(6 % 2): In this line, the code calculates the result of 6 modulo 2, which is the remainder when 6 is divided by 2. Since 6 is evenly divisible by 2, there is no remainder, and the result is 0. The comment # return 0 provides additional information about the expected output.

2. print(7 % 2): In this line, the code calculates the result of 7 modulo 2, which is the remainder when 7 is divided by 2. When 7 is divided by 2, it results in 3 with a remainder of 1. Therefore, the result of 7 % 2 is 1, indicating that there is a remainder of 1 when dividing 7 by 2. The comment #

return 1 provides additional information about the expected output.

In summary, the modulo operator % is used to find the remainder of division between two numbers. In the first case, where 6 is divided by 2, there is no remainder, so 6 % 2 returns 0. In the second case, where 7 is divided by 2, there is a remainder of 1, so 7 % 2 returns 1.

Exercise output only even numbers into the terminal

This example will output only the values that are matching the conditions. Using the % will check for a remainder, and if there is no remainder then it will continue the loop.

1. set a starting value for i
2. Create the loop to loop 10 times.
3. Increment that value of i
4. Add a condition to check if the value of i has a remainder using the %2, if it does its not even, add the continue statement.
5. print the value of i

```
i = 0
while i < 10:
    i=i+1
```

```
    if i%2:
        continue
    print(i)
```

While loops can have an else statement to run a block of code after the while loop completes. The below code will write the message "val is no longer less than 11" once the condition of the while loop val <= 10 is no longer true, and print "val is no longer less than 11" once it's completed.

```
val = 0
while val <= 10:
   print(val)
   val += 1
   if val == 2:
       continue
   if val == 15:
       break
else:
   print("val is no longer less than 11")
```

This Python code demonstrates the use of a while loop with the continue and break statements. It prints numbers from 0 to 10 using a while loop and applies conditional statements to control the loop's behavior. Here's a step-by-step explanation of the code:

1. val = 0: This line initializes the variable val to 0. This variable will be used as a counter in the loop.

2. while val <= 10:: This line starts a while loop. The loop continues as long as the value of val is less than or equal to 10.

3. print(val): Inside the loop, this line prints the current value of val during each iteration of the loop.

4. val += 1: This line increments the value of val by 1 in each iteration, effectively counting up from 0 to 10.

5. if val == 2: continue: This if statement checks if the value of val is equal to 2. If it is, the continue statement is executed. The continue statement skips the rest of the current iteration and jumps to the next iteration of the loop.

6. if val == 15: break: This if statement checks if the value of val is equal to 15. If it is, the break statement is executed. The break statement immediately exits the loop, even if the loop condition (i.e., val <= 10) is still true.

7. else:: This is an optional else block associated with the while loop. It is executed when the loop condition becomes False, i.e., when val is no longer less than or equal to 10.

8. print("val is no longer less than 11"): Inside the else block, this line prints a message indicating that the loop has exited because val is no longer less than 11. This message will be printed after the loop finishes executing all iterations.

In summary, this code prints numbers from 0 to 10 while skipping the number 2 and exits the loop when val reaches 15. The else block is executed when the loop naturally terminates because the loop condition is no longer satisfied.

Using the string format output the current value of i in the terminal.

```
i = 0
while i < 10:
    str1 = 'Current value {}'.format(i)
    i+=1
    print(str1)
```

For loops can be used to iterate over a list of values or using a range can loop through the counter.

Below will output the values 0-9 in the terminal.
```
for i in range(10):
  print(i)
```

```
8   for i in range(10):
9       print(i)
10
```

PROBLEMS   OUTPUT   TERMINAL   DEBUG CONSOLE

```
0
1
2
3
4
5
6
7
8
9
```

Figure: Output from python code exercise

For loops are an excellent way to get the values contained in a list.

```
friends = ['Laurence','John','Jane','Lisa']
for friend in friends:
    print(friend)
```

The result of the above code is that the friends from the list are printed into the terminal.
The for can also loop through all the letters in a string

```
user = 'Laurence'
for letter in user:
    print(letter)
```

The break can be used to stop the loop. Below code adds a condition for the break if the letter is equal to u.

```
user = 'Laurence'
```

```
for letter in user:
    print(letter)
    if letter == 'u':
        break
```

Just as we saw in the while loop, continue can be used to skip the current iteration.

Exercise skip the letter e in the string

An example of how to loop through the letters of a string and apply a condition which affects the output.

1. create a string make sure at least one or more letters have an e

2. add a condition to continue if the value is e

3. print the result into the terminal.

```
user = 'Laurence'
for letter in user:
    if letter == 'e':
        continue
    print(letter)
```

This Python code demonstrates the use of a for loop to iterate through the characters of a string ('Laurence') and how to use the continue statement to skip a specific character when it matches a certain condition. Here's a step-by-step explanation of the code:

1. user = 'Laurence': This line initializes the variable user with the string 'Laurence'.

2. for letter in user: This line starts a for loop that iterates through each character in the user string. In each iteration, the current character is assigned to the variable letter.

3. if letter == 'e':: Inside the loop, this if statement checks if the current character (letter) is equal to the character 'e'.

4. continue: If the condition in the if statement is true (i.e., the current character is 'e'), the continue statement is executed. The continue statement immediately skips the current iteration of the loop and moves to the next character in the string.

5. print(letter): If the condition in the if statement is not true (i.e., the current character is not 'e'), this line prints the current character (letter). This means that all characters except 'e' will be printed.

   Here's what happens when the code is executed:
   - The for loop iterates through each character in the user string, starting with 'L'. Since 'L' is not equal to 'e', it is printed.
   - Next, the loop iterates to 'a', which is also not equal to 'e', so it is printed.
   - The loop continues to 'u', which is also printed.

- The loop then encounters 'e', and because of the if statement and continues, it skips printing 'e' and moves to the next character.
- Finally, the loop prints 'n', 'c', and 'E'.

So, the output of this code will be:

L
a
u
n
c
E

Notice that the character 'E' is printed in uppercase because string comparisons in Python are case-sensitive, and 'e' and 'E' are considered different characters.

Python functions

Functions are used to run a block of code, whenever the function is invoked, it runs the block of code. Functions can be reused, also can pass data into a function which is known as the function parameters. Information can be passed into the function as arguments contained within the parentheses. The function can have as many arguments as needed; they are separated with a comma. A function can also return a value which can be created within the function block of code.

Functions core part of programming, you can reuse blocks of code invoking them anytime within the code to run the function block of code. Function can have arguments that are values passed and assigned to the variable names used within the function arguments. These values can then be used within the function. You can also return values with functions, those values can then be assigned to variables and used within your Python Code.

A function is defined using the def keyword. The below code will output the word hello 3 times into the terminal.

```python
def sayHello():
    print('hello')
sayHello()
sayHello()
sayHello()
```

Using the arguments, a different value can be passed into the function and used within the block of code. The below example will loop through the friends list and output the friends name using the function code.

The variable that is passed into the function is available only within that block of code.

```python
def fun1(val):
    print(val*val)
fun1(1)
fun1(5)
fun1(6)
fun1(7)
```

Result will be as follows:

```
1
25
36
49
```

Variable Scope from Functions

The variables are scoped to the block of code. If a variable is set on the first level this is globally available. If a new variable is set within a block of code using the same variable name that value will be assigned to the new variable that will be available only within that block. Variables that are created on the first level, not inside any function blocks of code are known as global variables. These variables can be accessed within any scope. When a variable is created within a block of code, that variable is not available outside the function block, only within the current block. All the parent block variables are also available inside the child scopes.

```
a = 5
b =10
def test():
   a = 15
   print(a)
test()
print(a)

Result
15
5
```

```
1   val = 100
2   def funBlock():
3       val = 10
4       print(val)
5   print(val)
6   funBlock()
7   print(val)
```

PROBLEMS   OUTPUT   TERMINAL   DEBUG CONSOLE

```
webs-iMac:Python web$ python3 test.py
100
10
100
webs-iMac:Python web$ []
```

Figure: Python code with output

Exercise: scope of variable value

This example will demonstrate how the variable scope works, and how the new values are affected with the same variable name in different scopes.

1. Set a variable on the global scope.

2. Create a function that has a variable using the same name, assign a different value to it.

3. Within the function print() the value of the variable

4. Invoke the function in the next statement and output the variable into the terminal.

```python
val = 'Laurence'
def funBlock():
    val = 'James'
    print(val)
print(val)
funBlock()
print(val)
```

This Python code illustrates the concept of variable scope and demonstrates how the scope of variables can change within and outside a function. Here's a step-by-step explanation of the code:

1. val = 'Laurence': This line defines a global variable named val and assigns it the value 'Laurence'. This variable has global scope, meaning it can be accessed and modified from anywhere in the code.

2. def funBlock():: This line defines a function named funBlock.

3. val = 'James': Inside the funBlock function, this line defines a local variable also named val and assigns it the value 'James'. This variable has a local scope, which means it is only accessible within the funBlock function and does not affect the global val variable.

4. print(val): Inside the funBlock function, this line prints the value of the local val variable, which is 'James'.

5. print(val): Outside the funBlock function, this line prints the value of the global val variable, which is 'Laurence'. This is because the global variable val is accessible throughout the entire code.

6. funBlock(): This line calls the funBlock function, which prints the local val variable (i.e., 'James') when executed.

7. print(val): After calling the funBlock function, this line prints the value of the global val variable again, which is still 'Laurence'.

When you run this code, you will see the following output:
Laurence
James
Laurence
Here's a summary of the variable scopes in this code:

The global val variable is defined outside the function and can be accessed throughout the entire code.
The local val variable is defined inside the funBlock function and has scope limited to that function. It does not affect the global val variable.

This example illustrates the difference between global and local variable scopes in Python. When a variable is defined within a function, it has local scope and does not interfere with variables of the same name defined outside the function.

Function arguments can be used resulting in different outputs depending on the value that is provided in the argument.

```python
def sayHello(friend):
    print('hello, '+friend)
friends = ['Laurence','John','Jane','Lisa']
for friend in friends:
    sayHello(friend)
```

Result:
hello, Laurence
hello, John
hello, Jane
hello, Lisa

Arguments can have a default value set using the = sign within function statement.

```python
def greeting(person='Laurence'):
    print('Hi, '+person)
greeting('Jane')
greeting()
```

This Python code defines a function named greeting that takes an optional parameter person with a default value of 'Laurence'. The function prints a greeting message using the provided or default value for person. The code then demonstrates calling this function with both specified and unspecified values for the person parameter. Here's a step-by-step explanation of the code:

1. def greeting(person='Laurence'): This line defines a function named greeting with a single parameter, person. The parameter person is assigned a default value of 'Laurence'. If no value is provided when calling the function, it will use this default value.

2. print('Hi, '+person): Inside the function, this line prints a greeting message that includes the name of the person. It concatenates the string 'Hi, ' with the value of the person parameter.

3. greeting('Jane'): This line calls the greeting function with the argument 'Jane'. When the function is called with an argument, it overrides the default value of person. So, in this case, it prints "Hi, Jane" because 'Jane' is provided as an argument.

4. greeting(): This line calls the greeting function without providing any arguments. In this case, the function uses the default value of 'Laurence' for the person parameter. It prints "Hi, Laurence" because no specific value was provided.

When you run this code, you will see the following output:
Hi, Jane
Hi, Laurence

This code demonstrates the use of default parameter values in a Python function. It allows you to provide a default value for a function parameter, which will be used if the caller does not specify a value for that parameter. If a value is provided when calling the function, it overrides the default value.

Arguments can be received as the order they are provided or preset as values within the function scope using the assignment value.

```python
def counter(val1,val2,val3):
    print(val2)

counter(1,2,3)
counter(val2=1,val3=2,val1=3)
```

Result will output 2 and the second result will be 1

To return a value from the function, use the return statement.

```python
def fun2(first,last):
    print("Hi, " + first + " " + last)
    return first + " " + last
fun2("Laurence","Svekis")
fun2("Linda","Jones")
fun2("Mike","Smith")
myName = fun2("Laurence","Svekis")
print(myName)
```

This Python code defines a function called fun2 that takes two arguments, first and last, prints a greeting message using these arguments, concatenates them to form a full name, and then returns the full name as a string. The code then calls this function multiple times with different values and assigns the returned full names to variables. Here's a step-by-step explanation of the code:

1. def fun2(first, last):: This line defines a function named fun2 that takes two parameters, first and last.

2. print("Hi, " + first + " " + last): Inside the function, this line prints a greeting message that includes the first and last names provided as arguments. It concatenates these values with strings to form the message.

3. return first + " " + last: This line returns the full name as a string by concatenating first, a space character, and last.

4. fun2("Laurence", "Svekis"): This line calls the fun2 function with the arguments "Laurence" and "Svekis". Inside the function, it prints "Hi, Laurence Svekis" and returns the full name "Laurence Svekis", but this return value is not assigned to any variable or used further.

5. fun2("Linda", "Jones"): Similar to the previous line, this line calls the fun2 function with different arguments, "Linda" and "Jones", and prints "Hi, Linda Jones". Again, the return value is not assigned or used further.

6. fun2("Mike", "Smith"): Similarly, this line calls the fun2 function with different arguments, "Mike" and "Smith", and prints "Hi, Mike Smith". The return value is not assigned or used further.

7. myName = fun2("Laurence", "Svekis"): This line calls the fun2 function with the arguments "Laurence" and "Svekis" and assigns the return value "Laurence Svekis" to the variable myName.

8. print(myName): Finally, this line prints the value stored in the variable myName, which is "Laurence Svekis".

When you run this code, you will see the following output:

```
Copy code
Hi, Laurence Svekis
Hi, Linda Jones
Hi, Mike Smith
Hi, Laurence Svekis
Laurence Svekis
```

This code demonstrates the definition and usage of a function that prints a greeting message, concatenates strings to form a full name, and returns the full name as a string. It also showcases how to call the function with different sets of arguments and store and use the returned values.

Exercise: Simple Math question game

The example code will output math questions with full question and answer into the terminal.

1. Create a function that requires two arguments
2. Assign to a variable total the value of the two arguments added together.
3. Print the results, to convert the number data type into a string use the str() method.
4. Return the total result.
5. Create 2 numbers, using the function that was just created, pass in 2 numeric values assigning the returned result values to variables.
6. Output the values of the returned variables into the terminal.

```
def fun3(val1,val2):
    total = val1 + val2
    print(str(val1) + " + " + str(val2) + " =
" + str(total))
    return total
num1 = fun3(6,7)
num2 = fun3(126,2317)
print(num1, num2)
```

This Python code defines a function called fun3 that takes two arguments, val1 and val2, calculates their sum, prints a message showing the addition operation and the result, and then returns the total. The code then calls this function twice with different sets of values and prints the results. Here's a step-by-step explanation of the code:

1. def fun3(val1, val2):: This line defines a function named fun3 that takes two parameters, val1 and val2.

2. total = val1 + val2: Inside the function, this line calculates the sum of val1 and val2 and stores the result in the variable total.

3. print(str(val1) + " + " + str(val2) + " = " + str(total)): This line prints a message that shows the addition operation and the result. It converts the numbers to strings using str() to concatenate them with the "+" and "=" symbols.

4. return total: This line returns the value of total from the function.

5. num1 = fun3(6, 7): This line calls the fun3 function with the arguments 6 and 7, and the result is assigned to the variable num1. Inside the function, 6 + 7 is calculated, and the message "6 + 7 = 13" is printed.

6. num2 = fun3(126, 2317): This line calls the fun3 function with the arguments 126 and 2317, and the result is assigned to the variable num2. Inside the function, 126 +

2317 is calculated, and the message "126 + 2317 = 2443" is printed.

7. print(num1, num2): Finally, this line prints the values stored in the variables num1 and num2, which are 13 and 2443, respectively.

When you run this code, you will see the following output:
6 + 7 = 13
126 + 2317 = 2443
13 2443
This code demonstrates the definition and usage of a function that performs addition, prints informative messages, and returns a result. It also showcases how you can call the function with different sets of arguments and store and use the returned values.

Lambda functions
Shorter anonymous functions written as one statement and can only contain one expression.

```
val = lambda a : a * 5
num1 = val(10)
print(num1)
val1 = lambda a,b : a * b
num2 = val1(10,20)
print(num2)
print(val1(3,9))
```

This Python code demonstrates the use of lambda functions, also known as anonymous functions, to define and use simple functions without explicitly defining a named function using def. Here's a step-by-step explanation of the code:

1. val = lambda a : a * 5: This line defines a lambda function val that takes one argument a and returns the result of multiplying a by 5. In other words, it's a lambda function that multiplies its input by 5.

2. num1 = val(10): This line calls the lambda function val with the argument 10 and assigns the result to the variable num1. The lambda function calculates 10 * 5, so num1 will be 50.

3. print(num1): This line prints the value stored in the variable num1, which is 50.

4. val1 = lambda a, b : a * b: This line defines another lambda function val1 that takes two arguments, a and b, and returns the result of multiplying a by b. This lambda function multiplies two numbers together.

5. num2 = val1(10, 20): This line calls the lambda function val1 with the arguments 10 and 20 and assigns the result to the variable num2. The lambda function calculates 10 * 20, so num2 will be 200.

6. print(num2): This line prints the value stored in the variable num2, which is 200.

7. print(val1(3, 9)): This line directly calls the lambda function val1 with the arguments 3 and 9 and prints the result. The lambda function calculates 3 * 9, so this line prints 27.

In summary, this code demonstrates the use of lambda functions to create small, inline functions for specific tasks. In the first lambda function (val), it multiplies the input by 5, and in the second lambda function (val1), it multiplies two inputs together. The code then applies these lambda functions to different sets of arguments and prints the results.

Function scope

Values can be accessed locally with the block of code that is assigning the values. Each block of code has its own scope, the main block of code is called the global scope. You can use variables from the parent block scope, but you cannot update the variable values within the child scope. There are keywords to access and update the global scope, you can use global to reference the variable you want to use. That opens the variable up to be updated within the child scope. You can also use the keyword nonlocal to access the parent scope variables to update them within a child local scope.

In the below example the user variable is only available within the function block, if you try to use it outside the block scope it won't be found.

```
def myName():
    user = 'Laurence'
    print(user)
myName()
```

If a variable value is not found in the current scope, the code will look to the parent scope. This is why the global variables are always available. The example below shows a function nested within another function, it is accessing the variable from the parent scope.

```
def myName():
    user = 'Laurence'
    def seeName():
        print(user)
    seeName()
myName()
```

Just like the function looking to the parent scope, both child blocks have access to any variables set in the parent blocks. The below code will still output the values of first and last correctly even though both are set in different scopes.

```
first = 'Laurence'
def myName():
    last = 'Svekis'
    def seeName():
        print(first + ' ' + last)
    seeName()
```

```
myName()
```

This Python code demonstrates nested functions and variable scoping. It defines two functions, myName and seeName, and shows how variables are accessed within nested functions. Here's a step-by-step explanation of the code:

1. first = 'Laurence': This line defines a global variable named first and assigns it the value 'Laurence'. This variable has global scope, meaning it can be accessed from anywhere in the code.

2. def myName():: This line defines a function named myName.

3. last = 'Svekis': Inside the myName function, this line defines a local variable named last and assigns it the value 'Svekis'. This variable has local scope, which means it is only accessible within the myName function.

4. def seeName():: Inside the myName function, this line defines another nested function named seeName.

5. print(first + ' ' + last): Inside the seeName function, this line attempts to print the values of both the first and last variables. It accesses the first variable, which is defined in the outer (global) scope, and the last variable, which is defined in the parent myName function's scope.

6. seeName(): After defining the seeName function, this line calls the seeName function from within the myName function.

7. myName(): This line calls the myName function from the global scope.

When you run this code, you will see the following output:
Laurence Svekis
Here's an explanation of how the code works:

The first variable is defined in the global scope and can be accessed from any part of the code.
The last variable is defined in the myName function's local scope and can only be accessed within the myName function.
The seeName function, even though it is nested inside the myName function, can access both the global first variable and the last variable defined in the parent function's scope. This is an example of how inner functions can access variables from their outer enclosing functions.

In summary, this code illustrates variable scoping in Python and shows how nested functions can access variables defined in their enclosing functions.
A variable created within the main body of the code, is known as a global variable. It can be used by any of the child scopes. If you name a variable the same as from the parent scope then, that new value will be the value used within any child scopes from that point descending.

Global Keyword

If you need to use the global value of a variable, adding the global for the value will use the global value making the variable global.

In the example below, the user name will both be 'Laurence' within the function scope, but the second function tester2() will change the global value to Laurence using the keyword global.

```
user = 'John'
def  tester1():
        user = 'Laurence'
        print('test1 '+user)
def  tester2():
        global user
        user = 'Laurence'
        print('test2 '+user)
tester1()
print(user)
tester2()
print(user)
```

This Python code demonstrates variable scoping and the use of the global keyword to modify a global variable from within a function. It defines two functions, tester1 and tester2, and shows how they interact with the user variable. Here's a step-by-step explanation of the code:
1. user = 'John': This line defines a global variable named user and assigns it the value 'John'. This variable has global

scope, meaning it can be accessed and modified from anywhere in the code.

2. def tester1():: This line defines a function named tester1.

3. user = 'Laurence': Inside the tester1 function, this line defines a local variable also named user and assigns it the value 'Laurence'. These local variable shadows the global user variable within the scope of the tester1 function.

4. print('test1 ' + user): Inside the tester1 function, this line prints a message that includes the value of the local user variable. Since the local variable user is defined, it is used within this function.

5. def tester2():: This line defines another function named tester2.

6. global user: Inside the tester2 function, this line uses the global keyword to indicate that the user variable being referenced should refer to the global variable rather than creating a new local variable. This means that any changes made to user within tester2 will affect the global user variable.

7. user = 'Laurence': Inside the tester2 function, this line assigns the value 'Laurence' to the global user variable.

8. print('test2 ' + user): Inside the tester2 function, this line prints a message that includes the value of the global user variable, which was modified within the function.

9. tester1(): This line calls the tester1 function, which prints "test1 Laurence" because it uses the local user variable defined within the function.

10. print(user): This line prints the value of the global user variable, which is still "John" because tester1 did not modify the global variable.

11. tester2(): This line calls the tester2 function, which prints "test2 Laurence" because it modified the global user variable.

12. print(user): Finally, this line prints the value of the global user variable, which has been modified to "Laurence" by the tester2 function.

When you run this code, you will see the following output:
test1 Laurence
John
test2 Laurence
Laurence
This code demonstrates how variable scoping works in Python. The tester1 function creates a local variable with the same name as the global variable, while the tester2 function modifies the global variable using the global keyword.

Using the keyword nonlocal will refer to the parent scope for the variable value.

What will the result be for the below code:

```python
a = "test"
b = 0
def fun1(val):
    global b
    b = b + 1
    def fun2():
        global b
        nonlocal val
        b += 5
        val += 1000
        print(val)
    fun2()
    print(a)
fun1(100)
print(b)
```

This Python code demonstrates variable scoping using global and nonlocal keywords within nested functions. It defines two functions, fun1 and fun2, and uses global and nonlocal variables to modify values. Here's a step-by-step explanation of the code:

1. a = "test": This line defines a global variable a and assigns it the string value "test".

2. b = 0: This line defines another global variable b and initializes it with the value 0.

3. def fun1(val):: This line defines a function named fun1 that takes one parameter val.

4. global b: Inside the fun1 function, this line uses the global keyword to indicate that the variable b being referenced should refer to the global b variable rather than creating a new local variable. This allows fun1 to modify the global b variable.

5. b = b + 1: Inside fun1, this line increments the global variable b by 1. After this line, b becomes 1.

6. def fun2():: Inside the fun1 function, this line defines another nested function named fun2.

7. global b: Inside the fun2 function, this line uses the global keyword again to indicate that the variable b being referenced should refer to the global b variable.

8. nonlocal val: Inside the fun2 function, this line uses the nonlocal keyword to indicate that the variable val being referenced should refer to the val variable from the outer fun1 function's scope. This allows fun2 to modify the val variable from fun1.

9. b += 5: Inside fun2, this line increments the global b variable by 5. After this line, b becomes 6.

10. val += 1000: Inside fun2, this line increments the nonlocal val variable by 1000. After this line, val becomes 1100.

11. print(val): Inside fun2, this line prints the value of the nonlocal val variable, which is 1100.

12. fun2(): This line calls the fun2 function from within the fun1 function.

13. print(a): Inside fun1, this line prints the value of the global variable a, which is "test".

14. fun1(100): This line calls the fun1 function with the argument 100.

15. print(b): Finally, this line prints the value of the global variable b, which is 6.

When you run this code, you will see the following output:
1100
test
6
This code demonstrates how the global and nonlocal keywords can be used to access and modify variables in different scopes. The fun1 function modifies the global variable b and the nonlocal variable val, and the fun2 function accesses and modifies these variables accordingly.

Exercise Number Guessing Game

Using a while loop creates a game that allows the user to make a guess at the hidden value of a number.

1. Start off create secret number in a variable

2. Set a variable that will limit the number of guesses

3. Create a variable to hold the number of guesses made by the user.

4. Setup a while loop that compares guess value to the secret number

5. Print provide the user how many guesses they have left

6. Capture the input from the users guess as a integer

7. If the users guess is correct set the final message as a WIN

8. Provide feedback to the user if their guess incorrect guess was too high or too low

9. Increment the counter and check if the count is at the max guesses, if it is break from the while loop

10. Output the WIN or LOSE message to the player

```
num = 10
limit = 6
cnt = 0
playGame = False
guess = 0
while guess != num :
   print("You have "+str(limit - cnt)+"
left")
   guessFirst = input("Enter a Number : ")
   if(guessFirst.isnumeric()):
       guess = int(guessFirst)
       if guess == num : playGame = True
       if(guess > num):
           print("Wrong too high")
       elif(guess < num):
```

```
            print("wrong too low")
    cnt+=1
    if((limit-cnt) == 0 ):
        break
else:
    playGame = True
if(playGame):
    print("You Got it!")
else:
    print("You ran out of guesses it
was:"+str(num))
```

This Python code implements a simple number guessing game. It allows the user to guess a hidden number, and the program provides feedback on whether the guess is too high or too low. Here's a step-by-step explanation of the code:

1. num = 10: This line sets the variable num to the hidden number that the player needs to guess. In this case, it's set to 10.

2. limit = 6: This line sets the variable limit to the maximum number of guesses allowed, which is 6.

3. cnt = 0: This line initializes the variable cnt to keep track of the number of guesses made by the player.

4. playGame = False: This line initializes the variable playGame to False. This variable will be used to determine whether the player successfully guessed the number.

5. guess = 0: This line initializes the variable guess to 0, which will store the player's current guess.

6. The while loop is the main part of the game. It continues running until the player guesses the correct number (guess == num) or runs out of guesses ((limit - cnt) == 0).

a. print("You have " + str(limit - cnt) + " left"): This line prints the number of remaining guesses to the player.

b. guessFirst = input("Enter a Number : "): This line prompts the player to enter a number as their guess and stores it in the guessFirst variable.

c. if(guessFirst.isnumeric())::: This line checks if the input provided by the player is numeric.

d. guess = int(guessFirst): If the input is numeric, it converts it to an integer and assigns it to the guess variable.

e. if guess == num : playGame = True: If the player's guess matches the hidden number (num), it sets playGame to True, indicating a successful guess.

f. if(guess > num):: If the guess is higher than the hidden number, it prints "Wrong too high."

g. elif(guess < num):: If the guess is lower than the hidden number, it prints "Wrong too low."

h. cnt += 1: This line increments the cnt variable to keep track of the number of guesses made.

i. if((limit - cnt) == 0):: This line checks if the player has used up all their allowed guesses (when (limit - cnt) becomes 0).

j. break: If the player runs out of guesses, the break statement exits the while loop.

7. else:: This else block is associated with the while loop. It is executed when the while loop terminates naturally, meaning the player either guessed the correct number or ran out of guesses.

a. playGame = True: It sets playGame to True to indicate a successful guess.

8. if(playGame):: This line checks whether playGame is True, which means the player successfully guessed the number.

a. print("You Got it!"): If playGame is True, it prints "You Got it!" to congratulate the player.

9. else:: This else block is executed when playGame is still False, indicating that the player ran out of guesses.

a. print("You ran out of guesses it was:" + str(num)): It prints a message revealing the correct number to the player.

Overall, this code implements a basic number guessing game with a limited number of guesses, providing feedback to the player after each guess. If the player guesses the number correctly or runs out of guesses, the game informs them of the outcome.

Try out what you've learned in this chapter, in order to be ready to move to the next chapter where more complex data objects will be introduced. This chapter covered the fundamentals needed to write code, these are the foundation for developing coding skills. The following chapters will provide more syntax that can be used to accomplish even more with code.

Chapter 3 Create with Python

Handling of data is an important part of coding, as it provides coders a way to better manage larger data, and interact with that data. Storing related values together within the same grouping is helpful in keeping code organized. As applications grow in scale they need more information and need to be able to manage the information better. This chapter will be introducing more useful container data types that can be used to store and access more values in a convenient way. In the upcoming lessons, we will be covering these larger data containers, and how they can be used within Python coding. Depending on the application requirements, and how the data will be used, can help determine which data type should be selected.

This chapter includes several exercises to practice using the data containers. As you go through the upcoming lessons, try the code to create your own version of the application so that you can get a feel for how the code works. It's important to practice and try the code.

Storing a collection of objects in Python

Variables can be used to reference a collection of objects in Python, there are four built in data types that can be used to store multiple items.

Python Lists are used to store multiple items, grouping them so that you can use one variable to reference the values. Lists are created with square brackets[].

Lists can be used to store multiple values to the variable. Lists contain several useful methods that can be used to update and interact with the contents of the list. Lists are created with square brackets that assign the value of the list to the variable. Example testList = [50,"100",True,50,"50"]

The List has a defined order and the order does not change when in the list. They will always have the same index value and the values can then be referenced using that index value. Within the list you can add new items and remove items from the list. There are several methods to manipulate the list contents that can be used for this. The list can be changed with methods or by selecting the item using the index value and assigning new values to it. You cannot have duplicate values which are allowed within the list. Use index value to identify and retrieve values from within the List each item will have its own index value depending on where the item is contained within the list order. Indexes are zero based, values start at zero so the first item in the list will have an index value or 0 and the second will be 1. You can use the len() function to determine the number of items within the list. A numeric value of the count of all the items in the list will be returned using the len() method.

List items have index values as the key to reference the value. Starting at zero for the first item in the list the index values increase to represent the items contained in the list. List items can be made up of any data type, and items can also be of different data types.

Lists can be used to sequence data types, and items can have various different data types. Lists are mutable, which means that the lists can be modified, updated and changed.

Return values from a list

To return a value from a list you can use the index value, state the list variable name, and directly next to it use the square bracket with the index value of the value you want to return from the list values.

```
list1 = ['a','b','c',1,2,3,True]
print(list1[0])
print(list1[4])
```

This Python code demonstrates the creation of a list called list1 and how to access its elements using indexing. Here's a step-by-step explanation of the code:

1. list1 = ['a', 'b', 'c', 1, 2, 3, True]: This line initializes a list named list1 that contains a mix of different data types, including strings ('a', 'b', 'c'), integers (1, 2, 3), and a boolean (True). Lists in Python can hold elements of different types.

2. print(list1[0]): This line prints the first element of the list list1 using indexing. In Python, indexing starts at 0, so list1[0] refers to the first element of the list, which is 'a'.

3. print(list1[4]): This line prints the fifth element of the list list1. Again, indexing starts at 0, so list1[4] refers to the fifth element, which is 2.

When you run this code, you will see the following output:
a
2
Here's a breakdown of the printed values:
- print(list1[0]) prints the first element of list1, which is 'a'.

- print(list1[4]) prints the fifth element of list1, which is 2.

  This code demonstrates how to create a list in Python, access its elements using square brackets and zero-based indexing, and print the values of specific elements within the list.

  Just as we can return the value, the value within the item can also be set using the index. Use the list and index value to assign new values to the list item. Below code will assign a value of Laurence to the first item in the list.

```
list1[0] = 'Laurence'
```

  Negative indexing can also be used to retrieve a value, with the negative index value it starts from the end of the list and moves towards the start. An index value of -1 will return the last item in the list as 0 would be the first item in the list.

```
list1 = ['a','b','c']
print(list1[1])
print(list1[-1])
```

  Result output :
  b
  c

  A range of values can also be returned from a list, selecting the starting index value and using a colon, with the end index value. This will not include the end index value item. If no starting value for the index is provided, the entire list items up until the second index value will be returned. If no ending index value is provided it will return all the results until the end of the list. This can be used to slice the values of the list, using the index values for the item positions.

```
list1 = ['a','b','c','d','e']
print(list1[:3])
print(list1[1:3])
print(list1[1:])
```

This Python code demonstrates how to use list slicing to extract specific portions of a list. The list list1 contains the elements 'a', 'b', 'c', 'd', and 'e'. Let's break down each line of code:

1. print(list1[:3]): This line uses list slicing to extract a sub-list from the beginning of list1 up to, but not including, the element at index 3 (exclusive). In other words, it includes elements at indices 0, 1, and 2. The result is ['a', 'b', 'c'].

2. print(list1[1:3]): This line uses list slicing to extract a sub-list starting from the element at index 1 (inclusive) up to, but not including, the element at index 3 (exclusive). It includes elements at indices 1 and 2. The result is ['b', 'c'].

3. print(list1[1:]): This line uses list slicing to extract a sub-list starting from the element at index 1 (inclusive) and continuing to the end of the list. It includes elements at indices 1, 2, 3, and 4. The result is ['b', 'c', 'd', 'e'].

When you run this code, you will see the following output:
['a', 'b', 'c']
['b', 'c']
['b', 'c', 'd', 'e']

In summary, list slicing is a powerful feature in Python that allows you to extract specific portions of a list by specifying the start and end indices. The syntax for list slicing is [start:end], where the start index is inclusive, and the end index is exclusive. If you omit the start index, it defaults to 0, and if you omit the end index, it defaults to the length of the list, allowing you to conveniently extract portions of a list.

Lists are ordered by index values. Ordered lists mean that they have a defined order, this would be represented by the index value. If you add a new item to the list it will be placed at the end of the list.

Duplicate values are allowed within the list as they will each have different index values.

Variables can be used within the list to assign a value to an item in the list. In the below example the list will have the value of name as the value of the first item in the list.

```
name = "Laurence Svekis"
testList = [name,50,"100",True,50,"50"]
```

Use the list name and index value to assign and retrieve the value at that index point in the list. Below code will assign a new value of NEW to index item 0 or first item in the list.

```
testList[0] = "New"
```

To get the last item in the list you can use -1 for the index. The below will return last item in the list

```
print(testList[-1])
```

To get a set of values from the list use the : to separate the start index and the end index value. Below will return the values starting at index 1 including that value and ending at index 3 not including index 3. The below will return the index value items starting at 1 and ending with 3 , if no end value is provided will return all the items until the end.

```
print(testList[1:3])
```

To return values starting at index 2 and listing all until the end of the list you can leave out the end value for index.

```
print(testList[2:])
```

To return all the results up to the index value but not including it you can leave out the start index. The below will return all expect the item with index 3

```
print(testList[:3])
```

Code Example :

```
testList =
["Laurence","World","Hello","World"]
a,b,c,d = testList
testList.insert(3,"Svekis")
testList.append("End")
testList.remove("Hello")
testList[0] = "New"
print(testList)
print(testList[1])
testList[1] = 'Updated'
print(testList[1])
print(testList[-1])
print(testList[2:3])
print(testList[2:])
```

```
print(testList[:3])
```

This Python code demonstrates various operations on a list named testList. Let's break down each part of the code:

1. testList = ["Laurence", "World", "Hello", "World"]: This line initializes the list testList with four elements: "Laurence," "World," "Hello," and "World."

2. a, b, c, d = testList: This line uses sequence unpacking to assign each element of testList to the variables a, b, c, and d. This means that a will be "Laurence," b will be "World," c will be "Hello," and d will be "World."

3. testList.insert(3, "Svekis"): This line inserts the string "Svekis" at index 3 in the testList. After this line, the list becomes ["Laurence", "World", "Hello", "Svekis", "World"].

4. testList.append("End"): This line appends the string "End" to the end of the testList. After this line, the list becomes ["Laurence", "World", "Hello", "Svekis", "World", "End"].

5. testList.remove("Hello"): This line removes the first occurrence of the string "Hello" from the testList. After this line, the list becomes ["Laurence", "World", "Svekis", "World", "End"].

6. testList[0] = "New": This line replaces the first element of the list with the string "New." After this line, the list becomes ["New", "World", "Svekis", "World", "End"].

7. print(testList): This line prints the entire modified testList.

8. print(testList[1]): This line prints the second element of the list, which is now "World."

9. testList[1] = 'Updated': This line replaces the second element of the list with the string "Updated."

10. print(testList[1]): This line prints the second element of the list, which is now "Updated."

11. print(testList[-1]): This line prints the last element of the list, which is "End."

12. print(testList[2:3]): This line uses list slicing to extract a sub-list containing the element at index 2 (inclusive) but not the element at index 3 (exclusive). In this case, it prints ['Svekis'].

13. print(testList[2:]): This line prints a sub-list starting from the element at index 2 (inclusive) to the end of the list.

14. print(testList[:3]): This line prints a sub-list from the beginning of the list to the element at index 3 (exclusive).

When you run this code, you will see the following output:
['New', 'Updated', 'Svekis', 'World', 'End']
Updated
Updated
End
['Svekis']
['Svekis', 'World', 'End']
['New', 'Updated', 'Svekis']
This code demonstrates various list operations, including insertion, appending, removal, replacement, slicing, and printing specific elements of the list.

Multiple values can be set in a list using the range, with a start and ending value for the index. The number of items inserted does not need to match the number being replaced, the list will adjust according to the values that are in the argument.

```
list1 = ['a','b','c','d','e']
list1[1:3] = ['B','C','D']
print(list1)
list1[1:4] = ['Laurence']
print(list1)
```

Output Result :
['a', 'B', 'C', 'D', 'd', 'e']
['a', 'Laurence', 'd', 'e']

To determine how many items in the list you can use the len() function, which will return the count of items in the list.

```
len(testList)
```

To get the data type the list can be set as an argument within the type() method which will return the type as 'list'

```
<type 'list'>
```

Update list values

When creating a list you can declare a list using the square brackets [] or use the list constructor to create the list. Both methods below will create a list with values, additionally if you want to create an empty list item values can be left blank.

```
list1 = ['a','b','c',1,2,3,True]
list2 = list(('a','b','c',1,2,3,True))
print(list1)
print(list2)
```

The provided Python code demonstrates two ways to create a list with the same elements. Let's break down each part of the code:

1. list1 = ['a', 'b', 'c', 1, 2, 3, True]: This line directly initializes a list named list1 with a combination of different data types, including strings ('a', 'b', 'c'), integers (1, 2, 3), and a boolean (True). The list elements are written explicitly within square brackets.

2. list2 = list(('a', 'b', 'c', 1, 2, 3, True)): This line creates a new list named list2 using the list() constructor. The constructor takes an iterable (in this case, a tuple) as an argument and converts it into a list. The tuple ('a', 'b', 'c', 1, 2, 3, True) contains the same elements as list1, and the list() constructor converts this tuple into a list.

3. print(list1): This line prints the contents of list1.

4. print(list2): This line prints the contents of list2.

When you run this code, you will see the following output:
['a', 'b', 'c', 1, 2, 3, True]
['a', 'b', 'c', 1, 2, 3, True]

Both list1 and list2 contain the same elements, and they are printed to the console. The first list, list1, is created using list literal notation, while the second list, list2, is created by converting a tuple into a list using the list() constructor. The result is two equivalent lists with the same elements.

To check if an item exists in a list, the keyword in can be used along with an if statement.

```
list1 = ['a','b','c','d','e']
if 'a' in list1:
    print('Yes')
else:
    print('No')
```

Result output :
Yes

Lists have methods that provide a way to interact and make use of the values contained within the list.

To add an item to the end of a list use append(). Insert() can also be used to add items to a list using the first parameter as the value of the index where the insert of items will be added. Insert only takes two arguments, the first is the index of the place where the new value will be inserted into the list.

```
list1 = ['a','b','c','d','e']
list1.append('f')
print(list1)
list1.insert(1,'B')
print(list1)
```

Output :
['a', 'b', 'c', 'd', 'e', 'f']

```
['a', 'B', 'b', 'c', 'd', 'e', 'f']

testList =
["Laurence","World","Hello","World"]
a,b,c,d = testList
testList.insert(3,"Svekis")
testList.append("End")
testList.remove("Hello")
testList[0] = "New"
print(testList)
```

This Python code demonstrates various operations on a list named testList. Let's break down each part of the code:

1. testList = ["Laurence", "World", "Hello", "World"]: This line initializes the list testList with four elements: "Laurence," "World," "Hello," and "World."

2. a, b, c, d = testList: This line uses sequence unpacking to assign each element of testList to the variables a, b, c, and d. This means that a will be "Laurence," b will be "World," c will be "Hello," and d will be "World."

3. testList.insert(3, "Svekis"): This line inserts the string "Svekis" at index 3 in the testList. After this line, the list becomes ["Laurence", "World", "Hello", "Svekis", "World"].

4. testList.append("End"): This line appends the string "End" to the end of the testList. After this line, the list becomes ["Laurence", "World", "Hello", "Svekis", "World", "End"].

5. testList.remove("Hello"): This line removes the first occurrence of the string "Hello" from the testList. After this

line, the list becomes ["Laurence", "World", "Svekis", "World", "End"].

6. testList[0] = "New": This line replaces the first element of the list with the string "New." After this line, the list becomes ["New", "World", "Svekis", "World", "End"].

7. print(testList): This line prints the entire modified testList.

When you run this code, you will see the following output:
['New', 'World', 'Svekis', 'World', 'End']
In summary, this code demonstrates various list operations, including insertion, appending, removal, and replacement. It also shows how to use sequence unpacking to assign list elements to variables.

Create a list of values, comma separate the values contained within the square brackets.

Using the insert() method will add an item into the list at a certain index value.

```
testList.insert(3,"Svekis")
```

Using the append() method will add an item at the end of the list.

```
testList.append("End")
```

Using the remove() method will remove the item with the selected value from the list.

```
testList.remove("Hello")
```

To remove items from the list use the remove() and the value of the item to be removed. Will remove the item from the list.

```
testList.remove("last1")
```

To remove the item and have it as a callback value, you can use pop() with the argument of the index value of the item. This will remove the item at index 1 and return the value in the statement. The value then can be assigned to a variable or output into the terminal with print(). With no index removes the last item in the list

```
print(testList.pop(1))
```

To select and delete an item at an index position use the del and the list item with index.
```
del testList[0]
```

To remove the entire list use del without an index.
```
del testList
```

To clear all the items out of a list you can use clear() Clear empties list contents.
```
testList.clear()
```

To sort the item order within a list use the sort() method. It sorts ascending and alphanumerically all the items within the list.
testList.sort()

```
['World1', 'Hello', 'World2']
['Hello', 'World1', 'World2']
```

To reverse order sort the list add a value of reverse = True
within the rounded brackets.

```
testList.sort(reverse = True)
```

Result would be:
['World1', 'Hello', 'World2']
['World2', 'World1', 'Hello']

To make a duplicate copy of a list use the copy() method.

```
copyList = testList.copy()
```

```
testList = ["Laurence","World1","Hello","World2"]
print(testList.index('Laurence'))
print("two" in testList)
testList.append("last1")
print(testList)
testList.insert(1,"last2")
print(testList)
testList.remove("last1")
print(testList)
print(testList.pop(1))
print(testList)
del testList[0]
print(testList)
#del testList
#testList.clear()
testList.sort(reverse = True)
print(testList)
copyList = testList.copy()
print(copyList)
```

This Python code demonstrates various list operations on a
list named testList. Let's break down each part of the code:

1. testList = ["Laurence", "World1", "Hello", "World2"]: This line initializes the list testList with four elements: "Laurence," "World1," "Hello," and "World2."

2. print(testList.index('Laurence')): This line uses the index() method to find and print the index of the first occurrence of the string "Laurence" in the testList. In this case, it prints 0 because "Laurence" is the first element in the list, and Python uses 0-based indexing.

3. print("two" in testList): This line checks if the string "two" is present in testList using the in keyword. Since "two" is not in the list, it prints False.

4. testList.append("last1"): This line appends the string "last1" to the end of testList. After this line, the list becomes ["Laurence", "World1", "Hello", "World2", "last1"].

5. testList.insert(1, "last2"): This line inserts the string "last2" at index 1 in testList. After this line, the list becomes ["Laurence", "last2", "World1", "Hello", "World2", "last1"].

6. testList.remove("last1"): This line removes the first occurrence of the string "last1" from testList. After this line, the list becomes ["Laurence", "last2", "World1", "Hello", "World2"].

7. print(testList.pop(1)): This line uses the pop() method to remove and print the element at index 1 of testList. It removes "last2" and prints it. After this line, the list becomes ["Laurence", "World1", "Hello", "World2"].

8. del testList[0]: This line uses the del statement to delete the element at index 0 of testList. After this line, the list becomes ["World1", "Hello", "World2"].

9. testList.sort(reverse=True): This line sorts the elements of testList in reverse order (descending). After this line, the list becomes ["World2", "World1", "Hello"].

10. copyList = testList.copy(): This line creates a copy of testList called copyList. Both lists have the same elements.

11. print(copyList): This line prints the contents of the copyList.

When you run this code, you will see the following output:
```
0
False
['Laurence', 'World1', 'Hello', 'World2', 'last1']
['Laurence', 'last2', 'World1', 'Hello', 'World2', 'last1']
['Laurence', 'last2', 'World1', 'Hello', 'World2']
last2
['Laurence', 'World1', 'Hello', 'World2']
['World2', 'World1', 'Hello']
['World2', 'World1', 'Hello']
```
This code demonstrates various list operations such as finding an element's index, checking for element existence, appending, inserting, removing, popping, deleting elements, sorting, and creating a copy of a list.

```
testList =
["Laurence","World1","Hello","World2"]
```

To remove items from a list use the remove() method and within the parenthesis as the argument use the value of the item you want to remove. Pop() can also be used to remove items from a list, in the argument you can add the index value of the item. If no index is provided, it will remove the last item from the list, the response back from the method will include the value of the item that was removed.

```
list1 = ['a','b','c','d','e']
list1.remove('a')
last = list1.pop()
first = list1.pop(0)
print(last)
print(first)
print(list1)
```

This Python code demonstrates various list operations on a list named list1. Let's break down each part of the code:
1. list1 = ['a', 'b', 'c', 'd', 'e']: This line initializes the list list1 with five elements: 'a,' 'b,' 'c,' 'd,' and 'e.'

2. list1.remove('a'): This line removes the first occurrence of the string 'a' from list1. After this line, the list becomes ['b', 'c', 'd', 'e'].

3. last = list1.pop(): This line uses the pop() method without an argument to remove and return the last element of list1. The removed element ('e') is assigned to the variable last. After this line, the list becomes ['b', 'c', 'd'].

4. first = list1.pop(0): This line uses the pop() method with an argument (0) to remove and return the element at index 0

of list1. The removed element ('b') is assigned to the variable first. After this line, the list becomes ['c', 'd'].

5. print(last): This line prints the value stored in the variable last, which is 'e,' the last element removed from the list.

6. print(first): This line prints the value stored in the variable first, which is 'b,' the first element removed from the list.

7. print(list1): This line prints the contents of the modified list1, which now contains only 'c' and 'd.'

When you run this code, you will see the following output:
```
e
b
['c', 'd']
```
In summary, this code demonstrates how to remove elements from a list using the remove() and pop() methods, and how to assign the removed elements to variables for further use. It also shows the resulting changes to the list after these operations.

Using the del keyword you can also remove items from the list. To delete the entire list, this can be done by using the del keyword and not providing any index.

```
list1 = ['a','b','c','d','e']
del list1[3]
print(list1)
```

Output:
['a', 'b', 'c', 'e']

List Methods

To clear the contents of a list use the clear() method.

```
people1 = ['Jack','Mike','Janet']
people1.clear()
print(people1)
```

This Python code demonstrates the use of the clear() method to remove all elements from a list. Let's break down each part of the code:

1. people1 = ['Jack', 'Mike', 'Janet']: This line initializes the list people1 with three elements: 'Jack,' 'Mike,' and 'Janet.'

2. people1.clear(): This line uses the clear() method to remove all elements from the people1 list. After this line, the list becomes empty.

3. print(people1): This line prints the contents of the modified people1 list, which is now empty.

When you run this code, you will see the following output:
[]
In this code, the clear() method is used to efficiently remove all elements from a list, resulting in an empty list. This can be useful when you need to reset or clear the contents of a list without recreating it from scratch.

List values can be sorted in place using the sort() method, and the reverse() method for the reverse sort order. These methods do not return any values, they update the list in place. The sort will be numbers first, then the letters alphabetically.

```
list1 = ['d',0,55,100,'a','b','c']
list1.sort()
print(list1)
list1.reverse()
print(list1)
```

This Python code demonstrates how to use the sort() and reverse() methods to modify the order of elements in a list. Let's break down each part of the code:

1. list1 = ['d', 0, 55, 100, 'a', 'b', 'c']: This line initializes the list list1 with a mix of data types, including strings, integers, and characters.

2. list1.sort(): This line uses the sort() method to sort the elements of list1 in ascending order. However, this will raise a TypeError because the list contains elements of different data types (strings and integers) that are not directly comparable.

3. print(list1): This line attempts to print the contents of list1 after the unsuccessful sorting attempt. Since sorting raised an error, the list remains unchanged.

4. list1.reverse(): This line uses the reverse() method to reverse the order of elements in list1. It doesn't perform a sort but simply reverses the existing order.

5. print(list1): This line prints the contents of list1 after the reverse operation. The list elements are now reversed.

When you run this code, you will encounter a TypeError when attempting to sort the list due to the mix of data types. However, the reverse() method successfully reverses the order of elements, resulting in the following output:
['c', 'b', 'a', 100, 55, 0, 'd']
In summary, the code demonstrates how to use the reverse() method to reverse the order of elements in a list. Sorting the list would require consistent data types or custom sorting criteria for mixed-type lists.

There are several ways to loop through the values contained within a list. Using the for in loop, will return the value which can then be used within the block of the loop.

```
people = ['Laurence','Jane','Joe']
for friend in people:
    print(friend)
```

This Python code demonstrates the use of a for loop to iterate over the elements of a list named people. Here's a step-by-step explanation of the code:

1. people = ['Laurence', 'Jane', 'Joe']: This line initializes the list people with three string elements: 'Laurence,' 'Jane,' and 'Joe.'

2. for friend in people:: This line starts a for loop. The loop iterates over each element in the people list one at a time, and for each iteration, the current element is assigned to the variable friend.

3. print(friend): This line prints the value of the friend variable during each iteration of the loop. As a result, it will print each name in the people list, one name per line.

When you run this code, you will see the following output:
Laurence
Jane
Joe
In summary, this code demonstrates how to use a for loop to iterate over the elements of a list. In this case, it prints each name in the people list, allowing you to process each element individually within the loop.

Another option for looping values contained within a list would be to use the while loop. Setting a starting value and providing a condition to break the loop. The increasing variable value can then be used as the index value of the array item.

```
people = ['Laurence','Jane','Joe']
i = 0
while i < len(people):
    print(people[i])
    i=i+1
```

Output Result :
Laurence
Jane
Joe

List reference and how lists work

If you assign a list to a new variable, that list will only be referencing the original list. This means any changes to the original list will also be in the new list. They are connected as the variable only references the list and unlike variables the actual value within the list. Since one list is assigned to another it will keep the reference in place and both lists will be the same list, assigned to two different variables. This is the same if you nest the existing list variable into a new list, any changes to the list will be reflected in both. This can get confusing and should be avoided.

```
people1 = ['Jack','Mike','Janet']
people2 = ['Laurence','Jane','Joe']
people3 = people2
people2[2] = 'Updated'
print(people2)
print(people3)
people1.append(people2)
print(people1)
people2[2] = 'NEW'
print(people1)
```

This Python code demonstrates the concepts of lists and variable references. Let's break down each part of the code:

1. people1 = ['Jack', 'Mike', 'Janet']: This line initializes a list people1 with three string elements.

2. people2 = ['Laurence', 'Jane', 'Joe']: This line initializes another list people2 with three different string elements.

3. people3 = people2: This line assigns the reference of people2 to the variable people3. This means that both people2 and people3 now refer to the same list in memory.

4. people2[2] = 'Updated': This line modifies the third element of the people2 list (at index 2) to 'Updated'. Since people3 also refers to the same list, it reflects the change as well.

5. print(people2): This line prints the contents of the people2 list, which is now ['Laurence', 'Jane', 'Updated'].

6. print(people3): This line prints the contents of the people3 list, which is also ['Laurence', 'Jane', 'Updated'] because people3 references the same list as people2.

7. people1.append(people2): This line appends the entire people2 list as a single element to the people1 list. Now, people1 contains four elements, and the last element is the people2 list.

8. people2[2] = 'NEW': This line modifies the third element of the people2 list (at index 2) to 'NEW'. This change does not affect people3 or the people1 list, as people1 contains a reference to the original people2 list at this point.

When you run this code, you will see the following output:
['Laurence', 'Jane', 'Updated']
['Laurence', 'Jane', 'Updated']
['Jack', 'Mike', 'Janet', ['Laurence', 'Jane', 'Updated']]
['Jack', 'Mike', 'Janet', ['Laurence', 'Jane', 'NEW']]

In summary, this code demonstrates how Python works with references to lists. Modifying the list through one reference affects all references pointing to the same list, but appending a list as an element to another list creates a new reference to the original list, making it independent of future changes to the original list.

To copy a list use the copy() method. This will create a copy of the list contents without connecting the lists. The list constructor can also be used to create a new list from an existing list.

```python
people1 = ['Jack','Mike','Janet']
people2 = ['Laurence','Jane','Joe']
people3 = people1.copy()
people4 = list(people1)
people1[0] = 'NEW'
print(people1)
print(people3)
print(people4)
```

This Python code demonstrates how to create copies of a list and the differences between different methods of creating those copies. Let's break down each part of the code:

1. people1 = ['Jack', 'Mike', 'Janet']: This line initializes a list people1 with three string elements.

2. people2 = ['Laurence', 'Jane', 'Joe']: This line initializes another list people2 with three different string elements.

3. people3 = people1.copy(): This line creates a shallow copy of the people1 list and assigns it to the variable people3.

This means that people3 now contains a new list with the same elements as people1, but it's a separate list in memory.

4. people4 = list(people1): This line also creates a shallow copy of the people1 list using the list() constructor and assigns it to the variable people4. Like people3, people4 now contains a new list with the same elements as people1.

5. people1[0] = 'NEW': This line modifies the first element of the people1 list to 'NEW'.

6. print(people1): This line prints the contents of the modified people1 list, which is now ['NEW', 'Mike', 'Janet'].

7. print(people3): This line prints the contents of the people3 list, which is a copy of the original people1 list and is not affected by the modification to people1. It remains ['Jack', 'Mike', 'Janet'].

8. print(people4): This line prints the contents of the people4 list, which is another copy of the original people1 list and is also not affected by the modification to people1. It remains ['Jack', 'Mike', 'Janet'].

When you run this code, you will see the following output:
['NEW', 'Mike', 'Janet']
['Jack', 'Mike', 'Janet']
['Jack', 'Mike', 'Janet']

In summary, this code demonstrates how to create copies of a list using the copy() method and the list() constructor, and how these copies are independent of the original list. Modifying the original list does not affect the copied lists.

Lists can also be concatenated together in several ways. To use the values from an existing list and add to a new list this can be done with the + to create a new list using the values of the lists.

To add the values of a list to another extend() method can also be used, it will add the values of the list within the argument to the list that has the method.

Both of these ways to use the values of a list, will provide a completely separated list of values between the lists. In the example below the list values are used in other lists with no reference to the list that contained the original values. They work independently of each other.

```python
people1 = ['Jack','Mike','Janet']
people2 = ['Laurence','Jane','Joe']
people3 = people1 + people2
people2.extend(people1)
people1[0] = 'NEW'
print(people1)
print(people2)
print(people3)
```

This Python code demonstrates various list operations, including concatenation, extension, and modification of lists. Let's break down each part of the code:

1. people1 = ['Jack', 'Mike', 'Janet']: This line initializes a list people1 with three string elements.

2. people2 = ['Laurence', 'Jane', 'Joe']: This line initializes another list people2 with three different string elements.

3. people3 = people1 + people2: This line concatenates people1 and people2 using the + operator and assigns the result to the people3 list. This creates a new list that contains all the elements from people1 followed by all the elements from people2.

4. people2.extend(people1): This line extends the people2 list by adding all the elements from people1 to it. After this line, people2 contains all elements from both people1 and people2.

5. people1[0] = 'NEW': This line modifies the first element of the people1 list to 'NEW'.

6. print(people1): This line prints the contents of the modified people1 list, which is now ['NEW', 'Mike', 'Janet'].

7. print(people2): This line prints the contents of the people2 list, which was extended to include the elements from people1. It is now ['Laurence', 'Jane', 'Joe', 'NEW', 'Mike', 'Janet'].

8. print(people3): This line prints the contents of the people3 list, which was created by concatenating people1 and people2. It contains the elements from both lists in the order in which they were concatenated.

When you run this code, you will see the following output:

['NEW', 'Mike', 'Janet']
['Laurence', 'Jane', 'Joe', 'NEW', 'Mike', 'Janet']
['Jack', 'Mike', 'Janet', 'Laurence', 'Jane', 'Joe']
In summary, this code demonstrates how to concatenate lists using the + operator, extend a list using the extend() method, and how modifications to one list do not affect the other lists that have been concatenated or extended.

The count() method provides a way to count the occurrences of the value in the list.

```python
people1 =
['Jack','Mike','Janet','Laurence','Jane','J
oe']
people2 = people1 + people1
people2.append('Laurence')
val1 = people2.count('Laurence')
val2 = people2.count('New')
print(people2)
print(val1)
print(val2)
```

This Python code demonstrates various list operations and the use of the count() method. Let's break down each part of the code:

1. people1 = ['Jack', 'Mike', 'Janet', 'Laurence', 'Jane', 'Joe']:

   This line initializes a list people1 with six string elements.

2. people2 = people1 + people1: This line concatenates people1 with itself using the + operator and assigns the result to the people2 list. This creates a new list containing all the elements from people1 followed by all the elements from people1 again, resulting in a list with twelve elements.

3. people2.append('Laurence'): This line appends the string 'Laurence' to the people2 list, so it now has thirteen elements.

4. val1 = people2.count('Laurence'): This line uses the count() method to count the number of occurrences of the string 'Laurence' in the people2 list and assigns the result to the variable val1. In this case, it will count how many times 'Laurence' appears in the list.

5. val2 = people2.count('New'): This line uses the count() method to count the number of occurrences of the string 'New' in the people2 list and assigns the result to the variable val2. Since 'New' is not present in the list, val2 will be assigned 0.

6. print(people2): This line prints the contents of the people2 list, which now contains thirteen elements, including two occurrences of 'Laurence'.

7. print(val1): This line prints the value of val1, which is the count of 'Laurence' in the people2 list. It will be the number of times 'Laurence' appears in the list.

8. print(val2): This line prints the value of val2, which is the count of 'New' in the people2 list. Since 'New' is not present in the list, it will be 0.

When you run this code, you will see the following output:
['Jack', 'Mike', 'Janet', 'Laurence', 'Jane', 'Joe', 'Jack', 'Mike', 'Janet', 'Laurence', 'Jane', 'Joe', 'Laurence']

3
0
In summary, this code demonstrates how to concatenate lists using the + operator, append elements to a list using the append() method, and count the occurrences of specific elements in a list using the count() method.

To get the index value of an item contained in the list you can use index() Below code will return a value of 0 which represents the index value of the item in the list that matched. The index() gets the index value of the item and will return the index numeric value.

```
print(testList.index('Laurence'))
```

To get a Boolean result you can use in. It will return a boolean result like in the below when the item is not in the list will be False.

```
print("two" in testList)
```

To add a new value to the end of a list use the append()

```
testList.append("last1")
```

Result :
['Laurence', 'World', 'Hello', 'World', 'last1']

To insert a new value into the list you can select the insert location by using the index value of where you want to insert it and then the value of what the item is that is being inserted. Below will insert a value at index 1 as last2 which will now be the second item in the list.

```
testList.insert(1,"last2")
```

Result:
['Laurence', 'last2', 'World', 'Hello', 'World', 'last1']

The index() method can be used to return the position of a value in the list. It returns the index position of the first occurrence of a specified value. If the value is not in the list then the result will cause an exception or ValueError.

```
people1 =
['Jack','Mike','Janet','Laurence','Jane','L
aurence','Laurence','Laurence','Laurence','
Joe']
val1 = people1.index('Laurence')
print(val1)
```

Output result:
3

Exercise: Loop through the contents of a List

The objective is to practice getting values contained within the list.

1. Create a list of names, do not capitalize the values
2. Loop through the list values and create a new list with the string values as capitalized values
3. Sort the names in the new list alphabetically
4. print the new list of names

```
people1 = ['jack','mike','janet','lAurence']
people2 = []
for person in people1:
```

```
    people2.append(person.capitalize())
people2.sort()
print(people2)
```

This Python code demonstrates how to create a new list based on an existing list, capitalize the strings in the new list, and then sort them alphabetically. Let's break down each part of the code:

1. people1 = ['jack', 'mike', 'janet', 'lAurence']: This line initializes a list people1 with four lowercase string elements, including names.

2. people2 = []: This line initializes an empty list people2. This will be used to store the capitalized versions of the names from people1.

3. for person in people1:: This line starts a for loop that iterates over each element in the people1 list. The current element is assigned to the variable person during each iteration.

4. people2.append(person.capitalize()): Inside the loop, this line capitalizes the current person string using the capitalize() method, which capitalizes the first letter of a string and makes the rest lowercase. The capitalized string is then appended to the people2 list.

5. After the loop completes, the people2 list contains the capitalized versions of the names from people1.

6. people2.sort(): This line sorts the elements in the people2 list in alphabetical order. The sorting is performed in-place, so people2 is modified.

7. print(people2): This line prints the contents of the people2 list, which now contains the capitalized names from people1, sorted alphabetically.

When you run this code, you will see the following output:
['Jack', 'Janet', 'Laurence', 'Mike']
In summary, this code demonstrates how to iterate over a list, apply a transformation to each element, and store the results in a new list. It then sorts the new list to get the capitalized names in alphabetical order.

The string method split will return a list of the string values. Once it's in a list format, the object can then be used with the list methods. Without a split() value in the argument, it will split the string by the spaces.

```
val = 'welcome to my page'
list1 = val.split();
print(list1)
```

Output
['welcome', 'to', 'my', 'page']

Exercise: Add Words that match a condition to new list

The following exercise is to start with a string, separate all the words from the string into a list. Then loop through the list of words, checking to see if the word contains a letter 'a'. If it does then add the word to a new list, which is printed out.

Exercise

1. Create a string with several words

2. split() the string into a list

3. loop through the list and check if the word contains a letter a

4. Add the word to the new list if it contains the letter a

5. print the new list to the terminal

```
val = 'welcome to my page thank you'
list1 = val.split();
list2 = []
for word in list1:
    if 'a' in word:
        list2.append(word)
print(list2)
```

This Python code demonstrates how to split a sentence into words and then create a new list containing only the words that contain the letter 'a'. Let's break down each part of the code:

1. val = 'welcome to my page thank you': This line initializes a string variable val with a sentence.

2. list1 = val.split(): This line splits the string val into a list of words using the default space (' ') as the separator. The resulting list, list1, contains all the words in the sentence.

3. list2 = []: This line initializes an empty list list2. This list will be used to store words from list1 that contain the letter 'a'.

4. for word in list1:: This line starts a for loop that iterates over each element (word) in list1. The current word is assigned to the variable word during each iteration.

5. if 'a' in word:: Inside the loop, this line checks if the letter 'a' is present in the current word. If it is, the following block of code is executed.

6. list2.append(word): Inside the loop, if the current word contains the letter 'a', it is appended to the list2 list.

7. After the loop completes, the list2 list contains only the words from list1 that contain the letter 'a'.

8. print(list2): This line prints the contents of the list2 list, which contains words containing the letter 'a'.

When you run this code, you will see the following output based on the input sentence:
['page']
In this example, the code identifies and extracts the word 'page' because it is the only word in the sentence that contains the letter 'a'.

List comprehension can provide a shorter syntax for the previous exercise, having it in one statement. The word variable can be used to represent the value from the list, and also the condition if met and true will then be returned, building a new list from the true results from the original list.

```
list3 = [word for word in list1 if 'a' in
word]
print(list3)
```

Result will output:
['page', 'thank']

This syntax can also be used on a string, to return all the
letters from the string into a list.

```
word1 = 'cat'
list4 = [char for char in word1]
print(list4)
```

output :
['c', 'a', 't']

Exercise : Word Letter Guessing Game

Letter guessing game, that will use a string value and ask
the player for input on guessing the secret words letters.
The gameplay will continue until all the letters of the secret
word are guessed. The objective is to practice working
with list data and applying methods to the data.

1. Set a string value of one word to a variable named word1

2. Using the word, create a list of the letters. Print the list into
    the terminal

3. Set a variable to calculate the misses, named miss and a
    value of 0.

4. Create a while loop to loop through while the list has a len greater than 0

5. create a variable to get the response from an input asking to guess a letter.

6. If the guessed letter is in the list, then get its index, and remove the letter from the list. Provide a feedback message to the user.

7. If the letter is not a value of one of the items in the list, increment the miss variable value, and provide feedback that the letter was not found.

```
word1 = 'cat'
list4 = [char for char in word1]
print(list4)
miss = 0
word1 = 'cat'
list4 = [char for char in word1]
print(list4)
miss = 0
while(len(list4) > 0):
    val = input('Guess a letter? ')
    if val in list4:
        ind = list4.index(val)
        list4.remove(val)
        print('Great found ' + val + ' at
index ' + str(ind))
    else:
        miss = miss + 1
        print('Not Found, ' + val + ', you
now have '+str(miss)+ ' letters missed.')
    print('There are ' +str(len(list4)) + '
letters left')
```

Output :
Guess a letter? w
Not Found, you now have 3 letters missed.
There are 3 letters left
Guess a letter? c
Great found c at index 0
There are 2 letters left
Guess a letter? a
Great found a at index 0
There are 1 letters left
Guess a letter? t
Great found t at index 0
There are 0 letters left

This Python code is a simple word guessing game where the player tries to guess letters in a word. Here's a step-by-step explanation of how the code works:

1. word1 = 'cat': This line initializes the variable word1 with the word to be guessed, which is 'cat'.

2. list4 = [char for char in word1]: This line creates a list list4 by using a list comprehension to iterate over each character (char) in word1 and store each character as an element in the list. After this line, list4 contains ['c', 'a', 't'].

3. miss = 0: This line initializes a variable miss to keep track of the number of incorrect guesses. It starts with a value of 0.

4. The code enters a while loop that continues until there are no letters left to guess (i.e., len(list4) becomes 0).

5. val = input('Guess a letter? '): This line prompts the player to enter a letter, which is stored in the variable val.

6. if val in list4:: This line checks if the guessed letter val is in the list4 (the remaining letters to be guessed).

7. If the guessed letter is in list4, the following block of code is executed:

a. ind = list4.index(val): This line finds the index (position) of the guessed letter val in list4.

b. list4.remove(val): This line removes the guessed letter val from list4.

c. print('Great found ' + val + ' at index ' + str(ind)): This line prints a success message indicating that the letter was found and at which index it was located.

8. If the guessed letter is not in list4 (i.e., it's a miss), the following block of code is executed:

a. miss = miss + 1: This line increments the miss count by 1.

b. print('Not Found, ' + val + ', you now have ' + str(miss) + ' letters missed.'): This line prints a message indicating that the letter was not found, how many misses the player has had, and which letter was guessed.

9. print('There are ' + str(len(list4)) + ' letters left'): This line prints the number of letters that are still left to be guessed.

The game continues until the player either successfully guesses all the letters in the word or exceeds a certain number of allowed misses (controlled by the miss variable). The game loop terminates when len(list4) becomes 0.

This code provides a simple text-based word guessing game where the player interacts with the program to guess letters in the word 'cat' while keeping track of misses.

Python Tuple

Tuple are created using rounded brackets testTuple = (50,"100",True,50,"50") The Tuple does allow duplicates since just like lists they are indexed. The order is defined and does not change. Within the items of the Tuple the allowed data types are strings, integers and booleans. It's also zero based; the first item in the Tuple will have an index of 0. Functions like len() can be used to retrieve the number or items contained in the Tuple.

Python Tuple is used to store multiple items into a single variable, although unlike lists Tuples are immutable objects which are unchangeable. Tuples are created using the rounded brackets (). Just like lists, the items in the Tuple can contain duplicate values.

```
tuple1 = ('Laurence','Lisa','Kim','Lisa')
print(tuple1)
```

Output
('Laurence', 'Lisa', 'Kim', 'Lisa')

Tuples also have methods, like the len() function to get the length count of the number of items within the tuple.

If the tuple only has one item, then it needs to be followed by a comma.

```python
tuple1 = ('Laurence',True,1000,'Lisa')
tuple2 = ('Laurence',)
print(len(tuple1))
print(len(tuple2))
print(type(tuple2))
```

This Python code demonstrates the creation of tuples and the use of the len() and type() functions to obtain information about them. Let's break down each part of the code:

1. tuple1 = ('Laurence', True, 1000, 'Lisa'): This line initializes a tuple tuple1 with four elements, which include a string, a boolean value (True), an integer (1000), and another string.

2. tuple2 = ('Laurence',): This line initializes a second tuple tuple2 with a single element, which is a string. The trailing comma is important to indicate that it's a tuple with one element; otherwise, it would be considered a string enclosed in parentheses.

3. print(len(tuple1)): This line uses the len() function to determine the length (number of elements) of the tuple1. It then prints this length. In this case, the length is 4 because there are four elements in tuple1.

4. print(len(tuple2)): This line uses the len() function to determine the length of tuple2, which contains one element. It prints this length, which is 1.

5. print(type(tuple2)): This line uses the type() function to determine the data type of tuple2 and then prints it. Since tuple2 is a tuple, it will print <class 'tuple'> to indicate that it is of type 'tuple'.

When you run this code, you will see the following output:
4
1
<class 'tuple'>
In summary, this code demonstrates how to create tuples in Python with different numbers of elements, how to use the len() function to determine the length of a tuple, and how to use the type() function to check the data type of a variable.

To return the results of the values from a tuple, it's the same syntax as was covered in the lists.

```
tuple1 = ('Laurence','Lisa','Kim','Lisa')
print(tuple1[:2])
print(tuple1[2:])
print(tuple1[2:3])
```

This Python code demonstrates various operations on tuples. Let's break down each part of the code:

1. tuple1 = ('Laurence', 'Lisa', 'Kim', 'Lisa'): This line initializes a tuple tuple1 with four string elements.

2. print(tuple1[:2]): This line uses slicing to create a new tuple containing the elements from index 0 (inclusive) up to index 2 (exclusive). In other words, it extracts the first two

elements of tuple1. The result is a new tuple, and it will print ('Laurence', 'Lisa').

3. print(tuple1[2:]): This line uses slicing to create a new tuple containing the elements from index 2 to the end of tuple1. It extracts the elements 'Kim' and 'Lisa'. The result is a new tuple, and it will print ('Kim', 'Lisa').

4. print(tuple1[2:3]): This line uses slicing to create a new tuple containing the elements from index 2 (inclusive) up to index 3 (exclusive). This means it will extract only one element, 'Kim'. The result is a new tuple, and it will print ('Kim',).

When you run this code, you will see the following output:
('Laurence', 'Lisa')
('Kim', 'Lisa')
('Kim',)
In summary, this code demonstrates how to use slicing to extract specific portions of a tuple. Slicing allows you to create new tuples containing selected elements from the original tuple based on their indices.

Tuples are not updateable, in order to update the values would need to be assigned as a list, updated and then reassigned to the tuple variable.

Values of the tuple can be unpacked as separate variables. The arguments in the list will return the items with the matching order from the tuple.

```
tuple1 = ('Laurence','Svekis')
```

```
(first,last) = tuple1
print(first)
print(last)
```

Output:
Laurence
Svekis

To loop through the values within a tuple you can use the for in loop, or the while loop.

```
tuple1 = ('a','b','c')
for str in tuple1:
    print(str)

i = 0
while i < len(tuple1):
    print(tuple1[i])
    i = i + 1
```

This Python code demonstrates two ways to iterate through the elements of a tuple. Let's break down each part of the code:

1. tuple1 = ('a', 'b', 'c'): This line initializes a tuple tuple1 with three string elements.

2. for str in tuple1:: This line starts a for loop that iterates over each element (str) in the tuple1. The loop will execute once for each element in the tuple.

3. print(str): Inside the loop, this line prints the current element (str) of the tuple. It will print each element one by one.

4. i = 0: This line initializes a variable i to 0. i will be used as an index to access elements of the tuple in the next part of the code.

5. while i < len(tuple1):: This line starts a while loop that continues as long as i is less than the length of tuple1.

6. print(tuple1[i]): Inside the while loop, this line prints the element of tuple1 at the current index i. It starts with i equal to 0 and prints the first element, then increments i by 1 to access the next element in the next iteration.

7. i = i + 1: Inside the while loop, this line increments the i variable by 1 in each iteration to move to the next element in the tuple.

When you run this code, you will see the following output:
a
b
c
a
b
c
In summary, this code demonstrates two ways to iterate through the elements of a tuple: using a for loop and using a while loop with an index variable. Both methods achieve the same result of printing each element of the tuple.

Python Dictionary

Dictionaries are used to store values, using a key for the value in a key:value pair. Dictionaries are changeable and do not allow for duplicate key values. Including a second identical key will overwrite the value for the previous reference value for the key. Dictionaries are written with curly brackets, using a name:value pair to set the items. Multiple values are comma separated just like we saw in the lists. Different data types can be set as the values, each key needs to be unique and set using the quotes around the key value. To assign a value to the key use the colon. You can use single or double quotes for the keynames.

Dictionary - named key value pairs using curly brackets
testDic =
{"first":50,"second":"100","third":True,"a":50,"a":"LAST"}
- order does not change as they are not indexed and

  accessed using the key value
- Can be changed and updated as needed referencing the

  key value. Add and remove new items into the dictionary
- Cannot have more than one item using the key name
- Dictionaries can contain nested dictionaries in a child

  parent format

There are two ways to create a new dictionary, either with the curly brackets {} or with the dict() method. Both methods are equivalent and will create a dictionary.

```
dict1 = dict()
dict2 = {}
```

```
print(dict1)
print(dict2)
print(type(dict1))
print(type(dict2))
```

This Python code demonstrates how to create empty dictionaries and obtain information about them. Let's break down each part of the code:

1. dict1 = dict(): This line creates an empty dictionary named dict1 using the built-in dict() constructor. In Python, dictionaries are collections of key-value pairs, and this line initializes an empty one.

2. dict2 = {}: This line creates another empty dictionary named dict2 using curly braces {}. This is an alternative way to create an empty dictionary, and it's more concise.

3. print(dict1): This line prints the contents of dict1. Since it's an empty dictionary, it will print {} to indicate an empty dictionary.

4. print(dict2): This line prints the contents of dict2, which is also an empty dictionary. It will also print {}.

5. print(type(dict1)): This line uses the type() function to determine the data type of dict1 and then prints it. It will print <class 'dict'> to indicate that dict1 is of type 'dict'.

6. print(type(dict2)): Similarly, this line uses the type() function to determine the data type of dict2 and prints it. It will also print <class 'dict'>.

When you run this code, you will see the following output:
{}
{}
<class 'dict'>
<class 'dict'>
In summary, this code demonstrates how to create empty dictionaries in Python using both the dict() constructor and curly braces {}, and it also shows how to check the data type of a variable using the type() function.

You can also set values when the dictionary is being created by adding them in as name pair values and comma separating them.

```
dictionary1 = {"first":"Hello
World","num":100,"num":200,"num":300,"boo":
True}
print(dictionary1)
```

output:
{'first': 'Hello World', 'num': 300, 'boo': True}

To return a value from the dictionary use the dictionary variable name and within the square brackets the key name.

```
dictionary1 = {"first":"Hello
World","num":100,"num":200,"num":300,"boo":
True}
print(dictionary1['num'])
```

Output :
300

Using the dictionary and the key name within the square brackets new values can be assigned to the keys.

```
dictionary1 = {"first":"Hello
World","num":100,"num":200,"num":300,"boo":
True}
print(dictionary1['num'])
dictionary1['num'] = 1
print(dictionary1['num'])
dictionary1['first'] = 'Laurence'
dictionary1['last'] = 'Svekis'
print(dictionary1)
```

This Python code demonstrates the creation and
manipulation of a dictionary. Let's break down each part of
the code:

1. dictionary1 = {"first": "Hello World", "num": 100, "num":
   200, "num": 300, "boo": True}: This line initializes a
   dictionary named dictionary1 with multiple key-value
   pairs. The keys are strings, and the values can be of
   different types. Note that the key "num" is repeated three
   times, which is not allowed in a dictionary. The later
   assignments to the same key will overwrite the earlier
   ones.

2. print(dictionary1['num']): This line prints the value
   associated with the key 'num' in the dictionary1. However,
   due to the repeated assignments, the value associated with
   'num' is 300, so it will print 300.

3. dictionary1['num'] = 1: This line assigns a new value of 1 to the key 'num' in dictionary1. This overwrites the previous value of 300.

4. print(dictionary1['num']): This line prints the updated value associated with the key 'num', which is now 1. It will print 1.

5. dictionary1['first'] = 'Laurence': This line assigns a new value of 'Laurence' to the key 'first' in dictionary1. This overwrites the previous value 'Hello World'.

6. dictionary1['last'] = 'Svekis': This line adds a new key-value pair to dictionary1, where the key is 'last' and the value is 'Svekis'.

7. print(dictionary1): This line prints the entire contents of dictionary1 after the modifications. It will display the updated dictionary with the new values and key-value pair.

When you run this code, you will see the following output:
300
1
{'first': 'Laurence', 'num': 1, 'boo': True, 'last': 'Svekis'}
In summary, this code demonstrates how to create, update, and manipulate dictionary key-value pairs in Python. It also highlights that dictionary keys must be unique, and assigning a new value to an existing key will overwrite the previous value.

To remove items from the dictionary use the pop() method, with the keyname, or to remove the last inserted item use the popitem() method. The del keyword with the keyname can also be used to remove an item from the dictionary. The clear() method can be applied to remove all the items from the dictionary to empty.

```python
dictionary1 =
{'one':'one','two':'two','first':'Laurence'
,'last':'Svekis','num':1}
dictionary1.pop('two')
dictionary1.popitem()
del dictionary1['one']
print(dictionary1)
dictionary1.clear()
print(dictionary1)
```

This Python code demonstrates various operations on a dictionary, including removing key-value pairs and clearing the entire dictionary. Let's break down each part of the code:

1. dictionary1 = {'one': 'one', 'two': 'two', 'first': 'Laurence', 'last': 'Svekis', 'num': 1}: This line initializes a dictionary named dictionary1 with several key-value pairs. The keys are strings, and the values can be of different types.

2. dictionary1.pop('two'): This line removes the key-value pair with the key 'two' from dictionary1. After this operation, the key 'two' and its associated value 'two' are removed from the dictionary.

3. dictionary1.popitem(): This line removes and returns an arbitrary (key, value) pair from dictionary1. In Python 3.7

and later, dictionaries are ordered, so it will typically remove the last item added to the dictionary. In this case, it removes one of the remaining key-value pairs.

4. del dictionary1['one']: This line uses the del statement to delete the key-value pair with the key 'one' from dictionary1. After this operation, the key 'one' and its associated value 'one' are removed from the dictionary.

5. print(dictionary1): This line prints the contents of dictionary1 after the removal operations. It will display the updated dictionary without the removed key-value pairs.

6. dictionary1.clear(): This line clears all the key-value pairs from dictionary1, effectively making it an empty dictionary.

7. print(dictionary1): This line prints the contents of dictionary1 after the clear() method is called. It will display an empty dictionary.

When you run this code, you will see the following output:
{'first': 'Laurence', 'last': 'Svekis', 'num': 1}
{}
In summary, this code demonstrates how to remove specific key-value pairs from a dictionary using methods like pop(), popitem(), and del, as well as how to clear all key-value pairs from a dictionary using the clear() method.

To return a list of the keys or values from the dictionary there are keys() and values() methods.

```
dictionary1 =
{'one':'one','two':'two','first':'Laurence'
,'last':'Svekis','num':1}
print(dictionary1.keys())
print(dictionary1.values())
```

Output:
dict_keys(['one', 'two', 'first', 'last', 'num'])
dict_values(['one', 'two', 'Laurence', 'Svekis', 1])

Check to see if a key exists within the dictionary.

```
dictionary1 = {
    "first": "Laurence",
    "last": "Svekis"
}
if "first" in dictionary1:
    print('Found first as a key')
    print('The value is
'+dictionary1['first'])
```

This Python code demonstrates how to check if a specific
key exists in a dictionary and, if it does, access and print
the corresponding value. Let's break down each part of the
code:

1. dictionary1 = {"first": "Laurence", "last": "Svekis"}: This line
   initializes a dictionary named dictionary1 with two key-
   value pairs. The keys are "first" and "last," and the
   corresponding values are "Laurence" and "Svekis,"
   respectively.

2. if "first" in dictionary1:: This line checks whether the key "first" exists in the dictionary1. The in operator is used to test for the presence of a key in the dictionary.

3. If the key "first" is found in dictionary1, the following block of code is executed:

a. print('Found first as a key'): This line prints a message indicating that the key "first" was found in the dictionary.

b. print('The value is ' + dictionary1['first']): This line accesses the value associated with the key "first" using dictionary1['first'] and prints it along with a message. This line prints the value associated with the "first" key, which is "Laurence."

When you run this code, you will see the following output:
Found first as a key
The value is Laurence
In summary, this code demonstrates how to check if a specific key exists in a dictionary using the in operator and, if the key is found, access and use the corresponding value.

Looping through the values of a Dictionary

Dictionaries have both keys and values, depending on what you want to return, you can use the keys to get the values, or return just values. There is also the items() method that returns the key and value of each item in the collection. The for in loop will return just the keys in the dictionary, these can then be used to reference the key within the dictionary variable to return the value. Using the keys() or values() method will return the corresponding results from each request.

```
dictionary1 = {"first": "Laurence", "last":
"Svekis"}
for key in dictionary1:
    print(key)
for key in dictionary1:
    print(dictionary1[key])
for key in dictionary1.keys():
    print(key)
for val in dictionary1.values():
    print(val)
for key,val in dictionary1.items():
    print(key,val)
```

This Python code demonstrates various ways to iterate through the keys and values of a dictionary. Let's break down each part of the code:

1. dictionary1 = {"first": "Laurence", "last": "Svekis"}: This line

    initializes a dictionary named dictionary1 with two key-

    value pairs. The keys are "first" and "last," and the

corresponding values are "Laurence" and "Svekis," respectively.

2. for key in dictionary1:: This line starts a for loop that iterates over the keys of dictionary1. In each iteration, the variable key will take on one of the keys in the dictionary.

3. print(key): Inside the loop, this line prints the current key key. It will print each key in the dictionary one by one.

4. for key in dictionary1: (second loop): This is the same as the first loop, and it reiterates over the keys of dictionary1. This loop is used to demonstrate different ways of accessing values.

5. print(dictionary1[key]): Inside the second loop, this line prints the value associated with the current key key by using dictionary1[key]. It prints each value in the dictionary corresponding to the keys.

6. for key in dictionary1.keys():: This line uses the keys() method to explicitly iterate over the keys of dictionary1. It achieves the same result as the first loop.

7. for val in dictionary1.values():: This line uses the values() method to explicitly iterate over the values of dictionary1. In each iteration, the variable val will take on one of the values in the dictionary.

8. for key, val in dictionary1.items():: This line uses the items() method to explicitly iterate over both keys and values of dictionary1. In each iteration, the variables key

and val will take on one key-value pair from the dictionary.

When you run this code, you will see the following output:
first
last
Laurence
Svekis
first
last
Laurence
Svekis
first
last
Laurence
Svekis
first Laurence
last Svekis
In summary, this code demonstrates various ways to iterate through the keys and values of a dictionary using for loops and dictionary methods like keys(), values(), and items().

Exercise : Dictionary keys and values

Dictionary data can be selected and looped through using several different methods. This exercise will help demonstrate the various options for iterating the dictionary items.

1. create a dictionary with several items

2. Using the for in print the key and the value from dictionary using the key

3. Print each value from the dictionary using the values() method

4. Print each key from the dictionary using the keys() method

5. Print each value and key using the items() method

```
testDic = {
  "first" : "Laurence",
  "last" : "Svekis",
  "allowed" : "True"
}
for key in testDic:
  print(key + ":" + testDic[key])
for val in testDic.values():
  print(val)
for val in testDic.keys():
  print(val)
for key,val in testDic.items():
  print(key,val)
```

This Python code demonstrates various ways to iterate through the keys and values of a dictionary named testDic. Let's break down each part of the code:

1. testDic = { "first" : "Laurence", "last" : "Svekis", "allowed" : "True" }: This line initializes a dictionary named testDic with three key-value pairs. The keys are "first," "last," and "allowed," and the corresponding values are "Laurence," "Svekis," and "True," respectively.

2. for key in testDic:: This line starts a for loop that iterates over the keys of testDic. In each iteration, the variable key will take on one of the keys in the dictionary.

3. print(key + ":" + testDic[key]): Inside the loop, this line prints the current key key, followed by a colon and the corresponding value obtained using testDic[key]. It prints each key-value pair in the dictionary.

4. for val in testDic.values():: This line uses the values() method to explicitly iterate over the values of testDic. In each iteration, the variable val will take on one of the values in the dictionary.

5. print(val): Inside the loop, this line prints the current value val. It prints each value in the dictionary.

6. for val in testDic.keys():: This line uses the keys() method to explicitly iterate over the keys of testDic. In each iteration, the variable val will take on one of the keys in the dictionary. Note that the variable name val is used here, which is not intuitive; it should be named something like key for consistency.

7. for key, val in testDic.items():: This line uses the items() method to explicitly iterate over both keys and values of testDic. In each iteration, the variables key and val will take on one key-value pair from the dictionary.

When you run this code, you will see the following output:

first:Laurence
last:Svekis
allowed:True
Laurence
Svekis
True
first
last
allowed
first Laurence
last Svekis
allowed True
In summary, this code demonstrates various ways to iterate through the keys and values of a dictionary using for loops and dictionary methods like values(), keys(), and items(). It prints both the keys and values in different formats.

Copy dictionary

Just as we saw with the lists, when you assign an existing dictionary to a new variable, that new dictionary will be referencing the original dictionary. Any changes or updates will be applied to both. To make a new instance of a dictionary there are several options, using either the copy() method, or the dict() to create a new instance.

```
dictionary1 = {"first": "Laurence", "last": "Svekis"}
dictionary2 = dictionary1
dictionary3 = dictionary1.copy()
dictionary4 = dict(dictionary1)
dictionary1['id'] = 1
print(dictionary2)
print(dictionary3)
```

```
print(dictionary4)
```

This Python code demonstrates how dictionaries are assigned and copied, and how changes to one dictionary can affect others. Let's break down each part of the code:

1. dictionary1 = {"first": "Laurence", "last": "Svekis"}: This line initializes a dictionary named dictionary1 with two key-value pairs. The keys are "first" and "last," and the corresponding values are "Laurence" and "Svekis," respectively.

2. dictionary2 = dictionary1: This line assigns dictionary1 to dictionary2. It means that dictionary2 is now referencing the same dictionary object as dictionary1. They are essentially two variables pointing to the same dictionary in memory.

3. dictionary3 = dictionary1.copy(): This line creates a shallow copy of dictionary1 and assigns it to dictionary3. The copy() method creates a new dictionary with the same key-value pairs as dictionary1. It's a separate dictionary object in memory.

4. dictionary4 = dict(dictionary1): This line also creates a shallow copy of dictionary1 using the dict() constructor and assigns it to dictionary4. It has the same effect as dictionary3 and creates a new dictionary object in memory.

5. dictionary1['id'] = 1: This line adds a new key-value pair to dictionary1. It inserts the key "id" with the value 1 into the dictionary.

6. print(dictionary2): This line prints the contents of dictionary2. Since dictionary2 references the same dictionary object as dictionary1, it will include the added key-value pair "id: 1".

7. print(dictionary3): This line prints the contents of dictionary3. Since dictionary3 is a separate copy of dictionary1, it will not include the added key-value pair "id: 1".

8. print(dictionary4): This line prints the contents of dictionary4. Like dictionary3, dictionary4 is a separate copy of dictionary1, so it also won't include the added key-value pair "id: 1".

When you run this code, you will see the following output:
{'first': 'Laurence', 'last': 'Svekis', 'id': 1}
{'first': 'Laurence', 'last': 'Svekis'}
{'first': 'Laurence', 'last': 'Svekis'}
In summary, this code demonstrates the difference between assigning a dictionary and creating copies of dictionaries. Assigning simply makes two variables reference the same dictionary object, while copying creates new, independent dictionary objects.

Dictionary methods

A second option to create and update dictionary values, is to use the update() method. It works the same as when you assign a new value using the bracket syntax. To retrieve a value from a dictionary you can use the bracket syntax or the get() method, both will return the result the same way.

```
dict1 = {}
dict1.update({'first': 'Laurence'})
dict1['last'] = 'Svekis'
print(dict1['first'])
print(dict1.get('last'))
```

Python Sets

Sets - created using curly brackets testSet = {50,"100",True,50,"50",50,100,100,"a"}
- no order they are unordered. They have no set order that they appear in.

- values cannot be changed after its set although you can add to it and remove from it

- Allowed data types are strings, integers, and booleans

Get Values
check if it exists using ("value" in testSet)
```
testSet.add("Last")
testSet.remove("Last")
testSet.pop() removes random item
```

```
testSet =
{"Svekis",100,True,"Svekis",100,"Laurence"}
testSet.add("New")
testSet.remove(100)
testSet.pop()
val = ("Svekis" in testSet)
print(testSet)
print(val)
```

This Python code demonstrates the use of a set, including adding and removing elements, using the pop() method, and checking for membership in a set. Let's break down each part of the code:

1. testSet = {"Svekis", 100, True, "Svekis", 100, "Laurence"}:

   This line initializes a set named testSet with several

   elements. Sets are unordered collections of unique

   elements, so duplicate values are automatically removed.

   The set contains the elements "Svekis," 100, True, and

   "Laurence."

2. testSet.add("New"): This line adds the element "New" to

   the testSet using the add() method. Sets ensure that

   elements are unique, so if "New" was already in the set, it

   wouldn't be added again.

3. testSet.remove(100): This line removes the element 100

   from the testSet using the remove() method. After this

   operation, 100 will no longer be in the set.

4. testSet.pop(): This line removes and returns an arbitrary element from the set using the pop() method. Since sets are unordered, it may remove any element from the set.

5. val = ("Svekis" in testSet): This line checks if the element "Svekis" is in the testSet using the in operator. It assigns the result to the variable val, which will be True if "Svekis" is in the set and False otherwise.

6. print(testSet): This line prints the contents of testSet after the operations. It will show the modified set with "New" added, 100 removed, and one arbitrary element removed by pop().

7. print(val): This line prints the value of the variable val, which is True if "Svekis" is in the set and False otherwise.

When you run this code, you will see the following output (note that the order of elements in the set may vary due to its unordered nature):
{True, 'Svekis', 'New', 'Laurence'}
True
In summary, this code demonstrates how to work with sets in Python, including adding and removing elements, using the pop() method to remove an arbitrary element, and checking for membership in a set.

Exercise :Create a Dynamic Shopping list

Shopping trips, using lists and dictionaries create a game where the objective is to buy stuff from the store and spend all the money.   Make sure there is enough feedback to the player so they understand what to do next.

1. create a dictionary named costs, with a list of store items, the keys are the items and the values are the costs of the items.

2. Print the costs dictionary to the terminal

3. Create a list using the keys() from the costs dictionary. Assign to a variable named menu.

4. Create an empty list named bag

5. Create an integer with a numeric value for money

6. Create a function named getInput() Within the function using a while loop, while it's True ask an input question which item? Once the user selects an existing item, return the result.

7. Create a second function named getTotal(), create a while loop that will return a numeric value for the amount of items to purchase.

8. Create a while loop that will continue until the money runs out.

9. Within the while loop, add instructions to guide the player. Get the item the player wants to purchase, using the getInput() function.

10. Get the total number of units to be purchased, using the getTotal() function

11. Check if the item is in the costs dictionary, if it is calculate the subtotal cost for the purchase of the items.

12. Subtract the subtotal from the money amount, if the money amount is equal to, or greater than zero then add the purchase items into the bag list.

13. Continue the game until the player has zero dollars left

14. Include instructions for the game play.

```
Results in the terminal
{'banana': 2, 'apple': 1, 'cake': 5, 'milk': 4}
['banana', 'apple', 'cake', 'milk']
Select an item from the store
Which Item cake
cost of cake is $5
How many? 2
10
['2 cake']
You have $10 left.
Select an item from the store
Which Item banana
cost of banana is $2
How many? 5
10
['2 cake', '5 banana']
You have $0 left.
```

```python
costs =
{'banana':2,'apple':1,'cake':5,'milk':4}
print(costs)
menu = list(costs.keys())
bag = []
money = 20
def getInput():
    while True:
        sel = input('Which Item ').lower()
        if sel not in menu:
            print(f'Please select from
{menu}')
        else:
            return sel

def getTotal():
    while True:
        sel = input('How many? ')
        if sel.isnumeric() :
            return sel
        else:
            print('Needs to be a number')

while money > 0:
    print('Select an item from the store')
    print(menu)
    item = getInput()
    print('cost of ' + item + ' is $' +
str(costs[item]))
    total = getTotal()
    if item in costs:
        subTotal = int(costs[item]) *
int(total)
        print(subTotal)
        money = money - subTotal
```

```
        if money >= 0 :
            bag.append(str(total) + ' ' +
    item)
        else :
            money = money + subTotal
            print('You did not have enough')
    print(bag)
    print('You have $' +str(money) + '
    left.')
```

This Python code simulates a simple shopping experience where a user can select items from a menu and add them to a shopping bag while keeping track of their budget. Let's break down each part of the code:

1. costs = {'banana': 2, 'apple': 1, 'cake': 5, 'milk': 4}: This line initializes a dictionary named costs where keys represent item names, and values represent their respective prices.

2. menu = list(costs.keys()): This line creates a list called menu containing the keys (item names) from the costs dictionary. This list represents the available items in the store.

3. bag = []: This line initializes an empty list named bag to store the selected items.

4. money = 20: This line sets the initial budget for the user to $20.

5. getInput(): This is a function that prompts the user to select an item from the store. It keeps asking until a valid item is chosen from the menu.

6. getTotal(): This is a function that prompts the user to specify the quantity of the selected item. It keeps asking until a valid number is entered.

7. The main shopping loop begins with while money > 0:. It continues as long as the user has a positive budget.

8. Inside the loop:

a. The available menu is displayed.

b. The user is prompted to select an item using getInput().

c. The cost of the selected item is displayed.

d. The user is prompted to enter the quantity using getTotal().

e. The code calculates the subtotal cost of the selected items and deducts it from the user's budget.

f. If the user has enough money, the item and quantity are added to the bag list. Otherwise, the money is restored, and a message is displayed.

g. The contents of the shopping bag and the remaining budget are displayed.

The loop continues until the user's budget is exhausted or they choose to exit.

When you run this code, you can interactively simulate a shopping experience. You can select items, specify quantities, and see the updated shopping bag and remaining budget as you shop.

The different data type containers can be used as needed within the structure of the code. Select the type that best suits the needs of the application and that matches the data that will be used. Consider how the data will be used and what will be required of it. In the upcoming chapter we will introduce more powerful features of coding, including methods, how to use classes and different data iterators.

Chapter 4 Python Classes and Objects

This chapter will cover the management of data and functionality, in regards to scope of the data and how it's handled. Previously we saw how functions can be used, that they can receive input, and produce a result in the output. Classes in Python provide a way to group data and functionality together. It creates a way that objects can be used as a structure that contain the attributes which can easily be recreated in new instances. Classes can be thought of as a blueprint for a future object that will be created based on it. Classes are a key ingredient to object oriented programming. This section will cover how to create classes, and reuse the class object.

Classes can be used to organize a data structure grouping data and methods, whereas functions can be used to perform specific action running the block of code. Classes make the code more readable and more efficient.

Print with variables

To output the values of variables into a print statement, without having to break from the string quotes, you can add the f tag prior to the string. Using the curly brackets include variables into the output result.

```
first = 'Laurence'
last = 'Svekis'
print(f'{first} {last}')
```

Output
Laurence Svekis

Within the curly brackets {} you can run Python code, to add numbers together or divide this can all be done within the print statement.

```python
print(f'{5+10} {9/2}')
```

Output
15 4.5

Global and nonlocal scopes, and namespaces

Assignments to variable names always go into the innermost scope, so if a creates a variable within an inner scope and the name is the same as a variable in the outer scope the variable that is inner will be used.

When we assign an object to a variable name, the name is bound to the object, which is not a copy of the data but a binding to the original object data. This was demonstrated in the previous section with the lists and dictionaries.

When creating variables on the global scope, that are available to all the scopes. When a variable is in the local scope it won't be available within the outer scopes, only scopes that are nested within it.

In the below example to assign the global scope to a variable, that can be done using the keyword global. For local scope this is done setting with the nonlocal keyword and the variable name. The inner value that is set to the variable of the same name, will not be used outside the scope. In the below example this is used in inner1(). The result for the inner1() is going to use the value that is set for the variable within the main() scope.

The local1() sets the nonlocal scope for the variable val, which indicates that the value of the variable is coming from the enclosing scope. This is why the output will show that value, but only within the main() scope. When local1() is invoked, it changes the value of val within the main() to be local 1

The global1() sets the global value, which is the value of the variable outside the main() scope. This is why the resulting value will be local 1 and not global 1 in the output. It's only when outside the main() scope that the global value of the val is set.

```
def main():
    def global1():
        global val
        val = 'global 1'

    def inner1():
        val = 'inner 1'

    def local1():
        nonlocal val
        val = 'local 1'
    val = 'Main 1'
    global1()
    print('Value 1 : ',val)
```

```
        inner1()
        print('Value 2 : ',val)
        local1()
        print('Value 3 : ',val)
    main()
    print('Value 4 : ',val)
```

This Python code demonstrates the use of different variable scopes, including global, local, and nonlocal, within nested functions. Let's break down each part of the code:

1. def main():: This line defines the main function, which serves as the entry point for the program.

2. def global1():: This line defines an inner function named global1().

3. global val: This line inside the global1() function declares the variable val as a global variable. This means that it will refer to the same variable val declared outside of any functions.

4. val = 'Main 1': This line initializes the global variable val with the string value 'Main 1'.

5. global1(): This line calls the global1() function. Inside global1(), it changes the value of the global variable val to 'global 1'.

6. print('Value 1 : ', val): This line prints the value of val after calling global1(). It will print 'global 1' because the global1() function modified the global variable.

7. def inner1():: This line defines another inner function named inner1().

8. val = 'inner 1': This line inside the inner1() function declares a local variable val and assigns it the value 'inner 1'. This local variable shadows the global variable val.

9. inner1(): This line calls the inner1() function. Inside inner1(), it changes the value of the local variable val to 'inner 1'.

10. print('Value 2 : ', val): This line prints the value of val after calling inner1(). It will print 'global 1' because the local variable val inside inner1() does not affect the global variable.

11. def local1():: This line defines yet another inner function named local1().

12. nonlocal val: This line inside the local1() function declares the variable val as nonlocal. This allows local1() to modify the variable val in the outer (main) function scope, not the global scope.

13. val = 'local 1': This line inside the local1() function assigns the value 'local 1' to the nonlocal variable val, which refers to the val declared in the main function.

14. local1(): This line calls the local1() function. Inside local1(), it changes the value of the nonlocal variable val to 'local 1' in the main function scope.

15. print('Value 3 : ', val): This line prints the value of val after calling local1(). It will print 'local 1' because the local1() function modified the nonlocal variable val in the main function scope.

16. main(): This line calls the main() function, initiating the execution of the program.

17. print('Value 4 : ', val): This line prints the value of the global variable val after calling main(). It will print 'local 1' because the local1() function modified the nonlocal variable val in the main function scope, and that change persists after the main() function call.

When you run this code, you will see the following output:

```
Value 1 :  global 1
Value 2 :  global 1
Value 3 :  local 1
Value 4 :  local 1
```
In summary, this code demonstrates the use of global, local, and nonlocal variables within nested functions and how each scope affects the value of the variable val.

Exercise Number Guessing Game

Using a while loop creates a game that allows the user to make a guess at the hidden value of a number.

1. Start off create secret number in a variable, create a function that will setup global values for the limit of guesses

2. Set a variable that will limit the number of guesses in the global setup() function

3. Invoke the setup() function to set the global values for the number to be guessed and the number of guesses that player will have.

4. Create a function for the game play playGame()

5. Create a variable to hold the number of guesses made by the user within the playGame() function. Setup a counter named cnt.

6. Setup a while loop that compares guess value to the secret number

7. Print provide the user how many guesses they have left

8. Capture the input from the users guess as a integer

9. If the users guess is correct set the final message as a WIN

10. Provide feedback to the user if their guess incorrect guess was too high or too low

11. Increment the counter and check if the count is at the max guesses, if it is break from the while loop

12. Output the WIN or LOSE message to the player

```
def setup():
    global limit
    limit = 6
```

```python
    global num
    num = 10

def playGame():
    guess = 0
    cnt = 0
    while guess != num  :
        print("You have "+str(limit - cnt)+"
left")
        guessFirst = input("Enter a Number :
")
        if guessFirst.isnumeric():
            guess = int(guessFirst)
            if guess > num:
                print("Wrong too high")
            elif guess < num:
                print("wrong too low")
        cnt+=1
        if limit - cnt == 0:
                print("You ran out of guesses
it was:"+str(num))
                break
    else:
        print("You Got it!")

setup()
playGame()
```

This Python code defines two functions, setup() and playGame(), and then uses them to simulate a simple number guessing game. Let's break down each part of the code:

1. def setup():: This line defines the setup() function. Inside this function, two global variables, limit and num, are declared and initialized.

2. global limit: This line declares the variable limit as a global variable. This means that it can be accessed and modified from outside the setup() function.

3. limit = 6: This line initializes the global variable limit with the value 6. limit represents the number of allowed guesses in the game.

4. global num: This line declares the variable num as a global variable. Like limit, it can be accessed and modified from outside the setup() function.

5. num = 10: This line initializes the global variable num with the value 10. num represents the target number that the player needs to guess in the game.

6. def playGame():: This line defines the playGame() function. Inside this function, the actual number guessing game logic is implemented.

7. guess = 0: This line initializes the guess variable to 0. The guess variable will be used to store the player's guesses.

8. cnt = 0: This line initializes the cnt variable to 0. The cnt variable will be used to keep track of the number of guesses made by the player.

9. The while loop (while guess != num:) is the core of the game. It continues until the player guesses the correct number or runs out of guesses.

a. Inside the loop, the remaining number of guesses is displayed to the player.

b. The player is prompted to enter a number as their guess.

c. The input is checked to ensure it is numeric using guessFirst.isnumeric().

d. If the input is numeric, it is converted to an integer and stored in the guess variable.

e. If the guess is higher or lower than the target number (num), appropriate messages are displayed to guide the player.

f. The cnt variable is incremented to keep track of the number of guesses made.

g. If the player has used all allowed guesses (limit - cnt == 0), a message is displayed, and the game breaks out of the loop.

10. The else block after the while loop is executed if the player successfully guesses the correct number within the allowed number of guesses. It prints "You Got it!" to indicate success.

11. setup(): This line calls the setup() function to initialize the game settings, including setting the limit and num.

12. playGame(): This line calls the playGame() function to start the number guessing game.

When you run this code, it simulates a simple number guessing game where the player has a limited number of guesses (determined by limit) to guess the target number (num). The game provides feedback on whether the guesses are too high or too low, and it informs the player if they've won or lost.

Python Class

Python is an object oriented programming language and objects play an important role in coding Python. Almost everything can be considered an object, with its own set of properties and methods.

Python classes provide a way to bundle data and functionality together. Classes create an object that can have instances of it created. Each instance can have the attributes of the main class attached to it. Class instances can also have methods which can be used to modify the state of the object.

Use the keyword class to create a class. The namespace for the class should be capitalized to indicate that this is a class.

```
class MyName:
    first = 'Laurence'
    last = 'Svekis'

user1 = MyName()
print(user1.first,user1.last)
```

Output Result :
Laurence Svekis

Methods the Class functions

Classes have built in functions that can be used within the class. All classes have a function called __init__() which gets executed when the class is initiated. This can be used to set up values that are contained within the class. Each class creates its own instance of the object. This is useful when creating multiple objects with the same structure.

In the example below the variable name main, is used to reference the current instance of the class. This allows for a reference variable that can then be used within other parts of the class instance to refer to the data contained within this particular class. Adding it to the main init() method, will set a way to access the values of the variables within the class scope.

The init method can be used to set default values and private variable values used within the scope of the object. These values will be set for each instance of the object and work independently. In the below example the code will create a private variable using the values of first and last that are set within the initial initiation of the object.

```
class MyName:
    def __init__(main, first,last):
        main.first = first
        main.last = last
        main.full = first + ' ' + last

user1 = MyName('Laurence','Svekis')
```

```
user2 = MyName('Jane','Doe')
print(user1.first,user1.last)
print(user1.full)
print(user2.full)
```

This Python code defines a class called MyName and creates two instances of that class, user1 and user2. Let's break down each part of the code:

1. class MyName:: This line defines a class named MyName.

2. def __init__(main, first, last):: This line defines the constructor method __init__ for the MyName class. The constructor is called when an instance of the class is created. It takes three parameters: main, first, and last.

a. main: This is a reference to the instance of the class (conventionally named self, but here named main).

b. first: This parameter represents the first name.

c. last: This parameter represents the last name.

3. Inside the constructor:

a. main.first = first: This line assigns the first parameter to an attribute named first of the instance (main).

b. main.last = last: This line assigns the last parameter to an attribute named last of the instance (main).

c. main.full = first + ' ' + last: This line creates a full name by concatenating the first and last names with a space in between and assigns it to an attribute named full of the instance (main).

4. user1 = MyName('Laurence', 'Svekis'): This line creates an instance of the MyName class named user1 with the first name 'Laurence' and the last name 'Svekis'. This instance will have first, last, and full attributes based on the constructor.

5. user2 = MyName('Jane', 'Doe'): This line creates another instance of the MyName class named user2 with the first name 'Jane' and the last name 'Doe'. Like user1, this instance will also have first, last, and full attributes based on the constructor.

6. print(user1.first, user1.last): This line prints the first and last names of user1.

7. print(user1.full): This line prints the full name of user1.

8. print(user2.full): This line prints the full name of user2.

When you run this code, you will see the following output:
Laurence Svekis
Laurence Svekis
Jane Doe
In summary, this code defines a class MyName with a constructor that initializes first name, last name, and full name attributes. It then creates two instances of the class and prints their attributes.

Custom Methods within a Class

Methods can be created within a class, and use the object data for that instance of the class. Methods are functions within the class that use the class scope and can be used within that instance. This provides a neater coding syntax when outputting the values from the class object data.

The example below has a function, which is known as a method within the class. This is not a default function but can be added to the object instance, and used to invoke the code within the method. In the below example create a method within the class to output the results of the main object data, when invoked it outputs the values into the terminal.

Within the init() method, variables can also be added to the main object data, for that instance of the class. In the case below, the counter is set up in the class, and then can be accessed within the instances of the class.

As in the previous example the full variable is created within the class instance. This variable can now be used within the instance.

```
class MyName:
    def __init__(main, first,last):
        main.first = first
        main.last = last
        main.full = first + ' ' + last
        main.counter = 0
    def makeFull(main):
        print('Full Name is ' + main.full)

user1 = MyName('Laurence','Svekis')
```

```
user2 = MyName('Jane','Doe')
user1.makeFull()
user2.makeFull()
```

This Python code defines a class called MyName with a constructor and a method. It then creates two instances of the MyName class and calls the makeFull() method on each instance. Let's break down each part of the code:

1. class MyName:: This line defines a class named MyName.

2. def __init__(main, first, last):: This line defines the constructor method __init__ for the MyName class. The constructor is called when an instance of the class is created. It takes three parameters: main, first, and last.

a. main: This is a reference to the instance of the class (conventionally named self, but here named main).

b. first: This parameter represents the first name.

c. last: This parameter represents the last name.

3. Inside the constructor:

a. main.first = first: This line assigns the first parameter to an attribute named first of the instance (main).

b. main.last = last: This line assigns the last parameter to an attribute named last of the instance (main).

c. main.full = first + '' + last: This line creates a full name by concatenating the first and last names with a space in between and assigns it to an attribute named full of the instance (main).

d. main.counter = 0: This line initializes a counter attribute to 0.

4. def makeFull(main):: This line defines a method named makeFull that takes a single parameter main. This method is used to print the full name of the person.

5. Inside the makeFull method:

a. print('Full Name is ' + main.full): This line prints the full name of the person using the full attribute of the instance.

6. user1 = MyName('Laurence', 'Svekis'): This line creates an instance of the MyName class named user1 with the first name 'Laurence' and the last name 'Svekis'.

7. user2 = MyName('Jane', 'Doe'): This line creates another instance of the MyName class named user2 with the first name 'Jane' and the last name 'Doe'.

8. user1.makeFull(): This line calls the makeFull method on the user1 instance, which prints the full name 'Laurence Svekis' to the console.

9. user2.makeFull(): This line calls the makeFull method on the user2 instance, which prints the full name 'Jane Doe' to the console.

When you run this code, you will see the following output:
Full Name is Laurence Svekis
Full Name is Jane Doe

In summary, this code defines a class MyName with a constructor that initializes first name, last name, and full name attributes. It also has a method makeFull that prints the full name of the person. Two instances of the class are created, and the makeFull method is called on each instance to print their full names.

The values of the objects can be updated, just as we saw with the dictionary the assignment of the object value can be changed with a new assigned value.

In the earlier example, the value of full was set on init, this created a set value for the full which was assigned at the initiation of the object. This value since it is set within the init, it will remain static and now update if the values of the first and last are updated. This is why it's best to make a custom method that will get the value of first and last at the time it's requested, and use those values to create the full name output.

In the below example the first name in the second instance will be changed to John. Keep in mind that the assignment of the full name when the class is initiated only occurs once, and that will still represent the original value. This can be updated with the reference to the object property name of full, not by updating the first or last name values of the object.

```
class MyName:
    def __init__(main, first,last):
        main.first = first
        main.last = last
        main.full = first + ' ' + last
        main.counter = 0
    def makeFull(main):
```

```
        print(f'Full Name is {main.first}
{main.last} originally {main.full}')
user1 = MyName('Laurence','Svekis')
user2 = MyName('Jane','Doe')
user2.first = 'John'
user1.makeFull()
user2.makeFull()
```

This Python code is similar to the previous example but
with a minor modification. It defines a class called
MyName, creates two instances of that class, and calls the
makeFull() method on each instance. Here's the breakdown
of the code:

1. class MyName:: This line defines a class named MyName.

2. def __init__(main, first, last):: This line defines the

    constructor method __init__ for the MyName class. The

    constructor is called when an instance of the class is

    created. It takes three parameters: main, first, and last.

a. main: This is a reference to the instance of the class

    (conventionally named self, but here named main).

b. first: This parameter represents the first name.

c. last: This parameter represents the last name.

3. Inside the constructor:

a. main.first = first: This line assigns the first parameter to an

    attribute named first of the instance (main).

b. main.last = last: This line assigns the last parameter to an

    attribute named last of the instance (main).

c. main.full = first + ' ' + last: This line creates a full name by concatenating the first and last names with a space in between and assigns it to an attribute named full of the instance (main).

d. main.counter = 0: This line initializes a counter attribute to 0.

4. def makeFull(main):: This line defines a method named makeFull that takes a single parameter main. This method is used to print the full name of the person.

5. Inside the makeFull method:

a. print(f'Full Name is {main.first} {main.last} originally {main.full}'): This line uses f-strings to print the full name, first name, and the originally stored full name of the person.

6. user1 = MyName('Laurence', 'Svekis'): This line creates an instance of the MyName class named user1 with the first name 'Laurence' and the last name 'Svekis'.

7. user2 = MyName('Jane', 'Doe'): This line creates another instance of the MyName class named user2 with the first name 'Jane' and the last name 'Doe'.

8. user2.first = 'John': This line modifies the first attribute of the user2 instance, changing it from 'Jane' to 'John'.

9. user1.makeFull(): This line calls the makeFull method on the user1 instance, which prints the full name 'Laurence

Svekis' and the originally stored full name 'Laurence Svekis' to the console.

10. user2.makeFull(): This line calls the makeFull method on the user2 instance, which prints the full name 'John Doe' and the originally stored full name 'Jane Doe' to the console.

When you run this code, you will see the following output:
Full Name is Laurence Svekis originally Laurence Svekis
Full Name is John Doe originally Jane Doe
In summary, this code defines a class MyName with a constructor that initializes first name, last name, and full name attributes. It also has a method makeFull that prints the current and originally stored full name of the person. Two instances of the class are created, and one of them modifies its first attribute before calling the makeFull method.

To delete the object use the keyword del.
The below code will throw an error since the value of the object has been deleted.

```
user1 = MyName('Laurence','Svekis')
del user1
user1.makeFull()
```

Object Values

When using a variable value, this can be done within the class, each instance of the class will have its separate value for the variable. If a variable is set in the class it will be available within that object scope.

The below example will create two separate instances of a counter, as the output() method is invoked the results for the counter variable value within the scope will be completely separate. The output method will print the results into the terminal.

```python
class Adder:
    def __init__(main):
        main.counter = 0
    def output(main):
        main.counter = main.counter + 1
        print('You requested this ' +
str(main.counter) + ' times')

add1 = Adder()
add2 = Adder()
count = 0
while count < 10:
    add1.output()
    count = count + 1
add1.output()
add2.output()
```

This Python code defines a class called Adder that has two methods: __init__ and output. It then creates two instances of the Adder class (add1 and add2) and calls the output method on them. Here's a breakdown of the code:

1. class Adder:: This line defines a class named Adder.

2. def __init__(main):: This line defines the constructor method __init__ for the Adder class. The constructor is called when an instance of the class is created. It takes one parameter, main, which is a reference to the instance of the class (conventionally named self, but here named main).

a. main.counter = 0: This line initializes an attribute named counter for the instance to 0. This attribute will be used to count how many times the output method is called on an instance of the class.

3. def output(main):: This line defines a method named output that takes one parameter, main. This method is used to increment the counter attribute and print a message indicating how many times it has been called.

a. main.counter = main.counter + 1: This line increments the counter attribute by 1.

b. print('You requested this ' + str(main.counter) + ' times'): This line prints a message that includes the current value of the counter attribute.

4. add1 = Adder(): This line creates an instance of the Adder class named add1.

5. add2 = Adder(): This line creates another instance of the Adder class named add2.

6. count = 0: This line initializes a variable count to 0, which will be used in the following loop.

7. while count < 10:: This line starts a loop that will execute as long as count is less than 10.

8. Inside the loop, add1.output() is called 10 times, and each time it increments the counter attribute of add1 and prints a message indicating how many times it has been called.

9. After the loop, add1.output() is called one more time, which increments the counter attribute of add1 again.

10. Finally, add2.output() is called, which increments the counter attribute of add2 and prints a message indicating that it has been called once.

When you run this code, you will see the following output:
You requested this 1 times
You requested this 2 times
You requested this 3 times
You requested this 4 times
You requested this 5 times
You requested this 6 times
You requested this 7 times
You requested this 8 times
You requested this 9 times
You requested this 10 times
You requested this 11 times
In summary, this code defines a class Adder with a constructor that initializes a counter attribute and a method output that increments the counter attribute and prints a message. Two instances of the class are created, and their output methods are called multiple times, resulting in different counters for each instance.

Exercise Separate counter exercise

Values of variables within the object are going to be separate from other instances of the object. This makes it possible to keep separate counts. This exercise will create several people, from the first and last name. It will count every time a request is made to see the full name of the person. The counter and the name will be displayed on each request.

Using a class creates two instances of people, with first and last names. Create a method that outputs the full name into the terminal, and counts the number of times the function has been invoked on each instance.

1. Create a class named MyName

2. In the class arguments provide a first and last name value

3. In init setup the counter and the full name value

4. Add a method named makeFull that uses the object values and increments the counter each time the method is invoked.

5. Output information to the user.

```
class MyName:
    def __init__(main, first,last):
        main.first = first
        main.last = last
        main.full = first + ' ' + last
        main.counter = 0
    def makeFull(main):
        print('Full Name is ' + main.full)
        main.counter = main.counter + 1
```

```
        print('You requested this ' +
    str(main.counter) + ' times')

    user1 = MyName('Laurence','Svekis')
    user2 = MyName('Jane','Doe')
    count = 0
    while count < 10:
        user1.makeFull()
        count = count + 1

    user1.makeFull()
    user2.makeFull()
```

This Python code defines a class called MyName that has a constructor method __init__ and a method makeFull. It then creates two instances of the MyName class (user1 and user2) and calls the makeFull method on them. Here's a breakdown of the code:

1. class MyName:: This line defines a class named MyName.

2. def __init__(main, first, last):: This line defines the constructor method __init__ for the MyName class. The constructor is called when an instance of the class is created. It takes three parameters: main, first, and last.

a. main: This is a reference to the instance of the class (conventionally named self, but here named main).

b. first: This parameter represents the first name.

c. last: This parameter represents the last name.

3. Inside the constructor:

a. main.first = first: This line assigns the first parameter to an attribute named first of the instance (main).

b. main.last = last: This line assigns the last parameter to an attribute named last of the instance (main).

c. main.full = first + ' ' + last: This line creates a full name by concatenating the first and last names with a space in between and assigns it to an attribute named full of the instance (main).

d. main.counter = 0: This line initializes a counter attribute to 0.

4. def makeFull(main):: This line defines a method named makeFull that takes a single parameter main. This method is used to print the full name of the person, increment the counter attribute, and print how many times it has been called.

a. print('Full Name is ' + main.full): This line prints the full name of the person using the full attribute of the instance.

b. main.counter = main.counter + 1: This line increments the counter attribute by 1.

c. print('You requested this ' + str(main.counter) + ' times'): This line prints a message indicating how many times the makeFull method has been called.

5. user1 = MyName('Laurence', 'Svekis'): This line creates an instance of the MyName class named user1 with the first name 'Laurence' and the last name 'Svekis'.

6. user2 = MyName('Jane', 'Doe'): This line creates another instance of the MyName class named user2 with the first name 'Jane' and the last name 'Doe'.

7. count = 0: This line initializes a variable count to 0, which will be used in the following loop.

8. while count < 10:: This line starts a loop that will execute as long as count is less than 10.

9. Inside the loop, user1.makeFull() is called 10 times, and each time it prints the full name, increments the counter attribute of user1, and prints how many times it has been called.

10. After the loop, user1.makeFull() is called once more, which increments the counter attribute of user1 again.

11. Finally, user2.makeFull() is called, which increments the counter attribute of user2 and prints how many times it has been called.

When you run this code, you will see the following output:
Full Name is Laurence Svekis
You requested this 1 times
Full Name is Laurence Svekis
You requested this 2 times
Full Name is Laurence Svekis
You requested this 3 times
Full Name is Laurence Svekis
You requested this 4 times
Full Name is Laurence Svekis
You requested this 5 times
Full Name is Laurence Svekis

You requested this 6 times
Full Name is Laurence Svekis
You requested this 7 times
Full Name is Laurence Svekis
You requested this 8 times
Full Name is Laurence Svekis
You requested this 9 times
Full Name is Laurence Svekis
You requested this 10 times
Full Name is Laurence Svekis
You requested this 11 times
Full Name is Jane Doe
You requested this 1 times
In summary, this code defines a class MyName with a
constructor that initializes first name, last name, and full
name attributes. It also has a method makeFull that prints
the full name of the person, increments the counter
attribute, and prints how many times it has been called.
Two instances of the class are created, and their makeFull
methods are called multiple times, resulting in different
counters for each instance.

Class Method Arguments

Just as with other functions, the method within the class
object can use parameters. Different arguments can be sent
into the method that can be used within the scope.

```
class Counter:
    def __init__(main,name,start):
        main.name = name
        main.start = start
    def adder(cur,val):
        cur.start = cur.start + val
```

```
        print(f'{cur.name} Points :
{cur.start}')

count = 0
counter1 = Counter('Laurence',0)
counter2 = Counter('Janet',10)
counter3 = Counter('Mike',11)
while count < 5:
    counter1.adder(2)
    counter2.adder(1)
    counter3.adder(4)
    count = count + 1
```

This Python code defines a class called Counter that has a constructor method __init__ and a method adder. It then creates three instances of the Counter class (counter1, counter2, and counter3) and calls the adder method on them in a loop. Here's a breakdown of the code:

1. class Counter:: This line defines a class named Counter.

2. def __init__(main, name, start):: This line defines the constructor method __init__ for the Counter class. The constructor is called when an instance of the class is created. It takes three parameters: main, name, and start.

a. main: This is a reference to the instance of the class (conventionally named self, but here named main).

b. name: This parameter represents the name of the counter.

c. start: This parameter represents the initial value of the counter.

3. Inside the constructor:

a. main.name = name: This line assigns the name parameter to an attribute named name of the instance (main).

b. main.start = start: This line assigns the start parameter to an attribute named start of the instance (main).

4. def adder(cur, val):: This line defines a method named adder that takes two parameters: cur and val. This method is used to increment the start attribute of the instance by val and print a message indicating the current points.

a. cur: This parameter represents the instance on which the method is called.

b. val: This parameter represents the value to be added to the start attribute.

   Inside the method:

c. cur.start = cur.start + val: This line increments the start attribute of the instance by val.

d. print(f'{cur.name} Points : {cur.start}'): This line prints a message that includes the name of the counter and its current points.

5. count = 0: This line initializes a variable count to 0, which will be used in the following loop.

6. counter1 = Counter('Laurence', 0): This line creates an instance of the Counter class named counter1 with the name 'Laurence' and an initial point value of 0.

7. counter2 = Counter('Janet', 10): This line creates another instance of the Counter class named counter2 with the name 'Janet' and an initial point value of 10.

8. counter3 = Counter('Mike', 11): This line creates a third instance of the Counter class named counter3 with the name 'Mike' and an initial point value of 11.

9. while count < 5:: This line starts a loop that will execute as long as count is less than 5.

10. Inside the loop, the adder method is called on counter1, counter2, and counter3, each with different values (2, 1, and 4, respectively). This increments their point values and prints messages indicating the current points.

11. count is incremented by 1 in each iteration of the loop.

When you run this code, you will see the following output:
Laurence Points : 2
Janet Points : 11
Mike Points : 15
Laurence Points : 4
Janet Points : 12
Mike Points : 19
Laurence Points : 6
Janet Points : 13
Mike Points : 23
Laurence Points : 8
Janet Points : 14
Mike Points : 27

In summary, this code defines a class Counter to represent counters with names and points. Instances of the class are created with different names and initial points, and the adder method is called on them in a loop to increment their point values and display their current points.

Class Inheritance

Python inheritance can be used to get all the methods and properties from another class. The parent class is the class that is used to inherit the methods and properties from. The child class is the class that will be inheriting the other class.

```python
class Username:
    def setup(main, first,last):
        main.first = first
        main.last = last
    def makeFull(main):
        print(f'Full Name is {main.first}
{main.last}')

class Friend(Username):
    def __init__(main, first,last,num):
        Username.setup(main, first,last)
        main.years = num
    def yearKnown(main):
        print(f'Known {main.first}
{main.last} for {main.years} years.')
user1 = Friend('Laurence','Svekis',10)
user1.makeFull()
user1.yearKnown()
```

This Python code defines two classes, Username and Friend, and creates an instance of the Friend class named user1. Here's a breakdown of the code:

1. class Username:: This line defines a class named Username.

2. def setup(main, first, last):: This line defines a method named setup for the Username class. The setup method is used to initialize the first and last name attributes of the instance.

a. main: This is a reference to the instance of the class (conventionally named self, but here named main).

b. first: This parameter represents the first name.

c. last: This parameter represents the last name.

3. Inside the setup method:

a. main.first = first: This line assigns the first parameter to an attribute named first of the instance (main).

b. main.last = last: This line assigns the last parameter to an attribute named last of the instance (main).

4. def makeFull(main):: This line defines a method named makeFull for the Username class. The makeFull method is used to print the full name of the person.

● main: This parameter represents the instance on which the method is called.

Inside the makeFull method:

- print(f'Full Name is {main.first} {main.last}'): This line prints the full name of the person using the first and last attributes of the instance.

5. class Friend(Username):: This line defines a subclass named Friend that inherits from the Username class. This means that the Friend class has access to the attributes and methods of the Username class.

6. def __init__(main, first, last, num):: This line defines a constructor method __init__ for the Friend class. The constructor is called when an instance of the Friend class is created. It takes four parameters: main, first, last, and num.

a. main: This is a reference to the instance of the class (conventionally named self, but here named main).

b. first: This parameter represents the first name.

c. last: This parameter represents the last name.

d. num: This parameter represents the number of years the person has known the friend.

7. Inside the __init__ method:

a. Username.setup(main, first, last): This line calls the setup method of the Username class to initialize the first and last attributes of the instance.

b. main.years = num: This line assigns the num parameter to an attribute named years of the instance (main).

8. def yearKnown(main):: This line defines a method named yearKnown for the Friend class. The yearKnown method is

used to print a message indicating how many years the person has known the friend.

a. main: This parameter represents the instance on which the method is called.

Inside the yearKnown method:

b. print(f'Known {main.first} {main.last} for {main.years} years.'): This line prints a message indicating how many years the person has known the friend using the first, last, and years attributes of the instance.

9. user1 = Friend('Laurence', 'Svekis', 10): This line creates an instance of the Friend class named user1 with the first name 'Laurence', last name 'Svekis', and a number of years known as 10.

10. user1.makeFull(): This line calls the makeFull method on user1 to print the full name.

11. user1.yearKnown(): This line calls the yearKnown method on user1 to print how many years the person has known the friend.

When you run this code, you will see the following output:
Full Name is Laurence Svekis
Known Laurence Svekis for 10 years.

In summary, this code defines two classes, Username and Friend, where Friend is a subclass of Username. Instances of the Friend class inherit the attributes and methods of the Username class and can also have their own attributes and methods. In this example, user1 is an instance of the Friend class and demonstrates the usage of both the inherited and custom methods and attributes.

Class pass

The keyword pass can be used when no additional properties or methods need to be added to the child class. If the class definition is empty then use the pass to avoid any errors.

```
class Friend:
    pass

person1 = Friend()
person1.first = 'Laurence'
person1.last = 'Svekis'
```

Exercise Friends List exercise add and update a list

Lists can be used within the class to create separate lists, with different methods. In the below exercise create a class that will create an instance of a list, that can be added to and removed from using the methods within the class.

1. Create a class named FriendList

2. Within the init, create a data list item that will be used to hold the friends list
3. Create a method to add a new person, append to the main object list the person's name, and print out the number of friends in the list.
4. Create a method to remove a person from the friends list. Print out the current list length.
5. Create a method to show the list of people in the current friends list instance.
6. Create an instance of the friend list class, add 3 names to the list. And remove one of those names
7. Show the people contained in the friends list.

```
class FriendList:
    def __init__(self):
        self.data = []
    def add(self, person):
        self.data.append(person)
        print(f'{person} added total friends
is now {len(self.data)}' )
    def remove(self,person):
        self.data.remove(person)
        print(f'{person} removed total
friends is now {len(self.data)}' )
    def show(self):
        print(self.data)

person1 = FriendList()
person1.add('Laurence')
person1.add('Jane')
```

```
person1.add('John')
person1.remove('John')
person1.show()
```

This Python code defines a class called FriendList, which is a simple implementation of a list to manage a list of friends. Here's an explanation of the code:

1. class FriendList:: This line defines a class named FriendList.

2. def __init__(self):: This is the constructor method for the FriendList class. It initializes an empty list called data when an instance of the class is created.

a. self: This parameter represents the instance of the class.

3. Inside the constructor (__init__) method:

a. self.data = []: This line creates an empty list named data as an attribute of the instance (self). This list will store the names of friends.

4. def add(self, person):: This method, named add, is used to add a friend's name to the list.

a. self: This parameter represents the instance of the class.

b. person: This parameter represents the name of the friend to be added.

   Inside the add method:

c. self.data.append(person): This line appends the person parameter to the data list, effectively adding the friend's name to the list.

d. print(f'{person} added total friends is now {len(self.data)}'): This line prints a message indicating that the friend has been added and the current total number of friends in the list.

5. def remove(self, person):: This method, named remove, is used to remove a friend's name from the list.

a. self: This parameter represents the instance of the class.

b. person: This parameter represents the name of the friend to be removed.

       Inside the remove method:

c. self.data.remove(person): This line removes the person parameter from the data list.

d. print(f'{person} removed total friends is now {len(self.data)}'): This line prints a message indicating that the friend has been removed and the current total number of friends in the list.

6. def show(self):: This method, named show, is used to display the list of friends.

a. self: This parameter represents the instance of the class.

       Inside the show method:

b. print(self.data): This line prints the contents of the data list, which are the names of friends.

7. person1 = FriendList(): This line creates an instance of the FriendList class named person1. person1 is an object that can store and manage a list of friends.

8. person1.add('Laurence'): This line adds the name 'Laurence' to the person1's friend list and prints a message indicating the addition.

9. person1.add('Jane'): This line adds the name 'Jane' to the person1's friend list and prints a message indicating the addition.

10. person1.add('John'): This line adds the name 'John' to the person1's friend list and prints a message indicating the addition.

11. person1.remove('John'): This line removes the name 'John' from the person1's friend list and prints a message indicating the removal.

12. person1.show(): This line displays the current list of friends stored in person1.

When you run this code, you will see the following output:
Laurence added total friends is now 1
Jane added total friends is now 2
John added total friends is now 3
John removed total friends is now 2
['Laurence', 'Jane']
In summary, the FriendList class allows you to add, remove, and display a list of friends. Instances of this class can keep track of the friends' names and perform basic operations on the list.

Return value Method

The class instance can receive argument values, and can also return values just like regular functions.

Exercise the Battle round

Simple mini battle game using classes to create instances of different players. Each player can have a different name, and power value. The power values are then used as the hit value for the following player. Within the class there is a method named battle() that is used to calculate the player status, including the health and the points. Health decreases by the hit amount, the points increase by the hit amount and the power from the player. The power and the hit amount are returned to the main game loop so that the following player can get the new results.

Exercise :
1. create a Player class, which has as init() arguments, the name of the player and the power. Each player should start with health of 100 and points of 0

2. Create a method that can be used for the battle. Pass in the main player object data as a variable, use user as the parameter name. Add a second parameter which will receive the hit amount argument.

3. In the battle() method, subtract the hit value from the player's health.

4. In the battle() method, add the hit multiplied by the player's power to the player's points.
5. Return the hit value back with the player power, to be used for the following player as the hit amount.
6. Using the class, create 3 players, with unique names and values for the power.
7. Create a while loop that will loop 4 times, starting at 1
8. Within the while loop, print the round as the count for the loop. Add the increment to the count for the loop to eventually be able to end.
9. Setup a variable named pw, this can be initially set to the count plus 1.
10. Start with player 1, send the pw value in as the agruemtn for battle(). Assign the returned value from the battle() method to the pw variable.
11. Do the same for player 2 and player 3 each time returning back a new value to be used in the following player hit.

```
class Player:
    def __init__(main,name,power):
        main.name = name
        main.power = power
        main.health = 100
        main.points = 0
    def battle(user,hit):
        user.health =  user.health - hit
        user.points = user.points + (hit *
user.power)
```

```
        print(f'{user.name} Health
:{user.health} Points : {user.points}')
        return user.power + hit
player1 = Player('Laurence',2)
player2 = Player('Lisa',4)
player3 = Player('John',1)
count = 1
pw = count + 1
while count < 5:
    print('Round #'+str(count))
    pw = player1.battle(pw)
    pw = player2.battle(pw)
    pw = player3.battle(pw)
    count = count + 1
```

Output results :
Round #1
Laurence Health :98 Points : 4
Lisa Health :96 Points : 16
John Health :92 Points : 8
Round #2
Laurence Health :89 Points : 22
Lisa Health :85 Points : 60
John Health :77 Points : 23
Round #3
Laurence Health :73 Points : 54
Lisa Health :67 Points : 132
John Health :55 Points : 45
Round #4
Laurence Health :50 Points : 100
Lisa Health :42 Points : 232
John Health :26 Points : 74

This Python code defines a class called Player that represents game characters with attributes such as name, power, health, and points. These players can engage in battles, where they can lose health and gain points. Here's an explanation of the code:

1. class Player:: This line defines a class named Player.

2. def __init__(main, name, power):: This is the constructor method for the Player class. It initializes the player's attributes when an instance of the class is created.

a. main: This parameter represents the instance of the class.

b. name: This parameter represents the player's name.

c. power: This parameter represents the player's power.

   Inside the constructor (__init__) method:

d. main.name = name: This line sets the name attribute of the instance to the provided name parameter.

e. main.power = power: This line sets the power attribute of the instance to the provided power parameter.

f. main.health = 100: This line initializes the player's health to 100.

g. main.points = 0: This line initializes the player's points to 0.

3. def battle(user, hit):: This is a method named battle that simulates a battle for the player.

a. user: This parameter represents the player who is involved in the battle.

b. hit: This parameter represents the damage inflicted in the battle.

Inside the battle method:

c. user.health = user.health - hit: This line decreases the player's health by the amount specified in the hit parameter.

d. user.points = user.points + (hit * user.power): This line increases the player's points based on the product of hit and the player's power.

e. print(f'{user.name} Health :{user.health} Points : {user.points}'): This line prints a message displaying the player's current health and points.

f. return user.power + hit: This line returns a value calculated from the player's power and the hit value.

4. player1 = Player('Laurence', 2): This line creates an instance of the Player class named player1 with a name of 'Laurence' and a power of 2.

5. player2 = Player('Lisa', 4): This line creates an instance of the Player class named player2 with a name of 'Lisa' and a power of 4.

6. player3 = Player('John', 1): This line creates an instance of the Player class named player3 with a name of 'John' and a power of 1.

7. count = 1: This line initializes a variable count to 1.

8. pw = count + 1: This line initializes a variable pw to count + 1.

9. A while loop:

a. while count < 5:: This loop iterates as long as the count is less than 5, simulating multiple rounds of battles.
b. Inside the loop:
c. print('Round #' + str(count)): This line prints the current round number.
d. pw = player1.battle(pw): This line simulates a battle involving player1 and updates the pw variable.
e. pw = player2.battle(pw): This line simulates a battle involving player2 and updates the pw variable.
f. pw = player3.battle(pw): This line simulates a battle involving player3 and updates the pw variable.
g. count = count + 1: This line increments the count variable to move to the next round.

In this code, three players (player1, player2, and player3) are created and participate in multiple rounds of battles. The players' health, points, and power are updated during each battle, and the results are printed for each round. The loop continues for five rounds in this example.

Python Iterators

Iterators provide a way to iterate moving through all the items in the available values.

The below example shows using a string as the iteration object, and then the for in loop to move through the values.

```
name = 'Laurence'
```

```
nameIter = iter(name)

for letter in nameIter:
    print(letter)
```

Using the iter() can return an iterator object of the value. Then we can use next() to move to the next item in the object.

```
name = 'Laurence'
nameIter = iter(name)
print(next(nameIter))
print(next(nameIter))
print(next(nameIter))
```

Class Iterator

Classes have a default iterator function, just like the init function. The iter is written def __iter__ and the next method within the class is def __iter__

This allows for the creation of iteration of the class object. Once the class instance is assigned, the iter() method can be used to create the iterable object.

Exercise Count Stepper

Using the class to set up a method for iteration, this example will demonstrate how to output the result of a stepped count. The arguments for the class object include a starting value, the ending value and the step value for incrementing the count.

1. Create the counter class, setting the value that will be used to count, starting at the start value minus the step value.
2. Set the step and end values for the object
3. Set the Method for iter as returning the current object data
4. In the iter method, increase the value of the counter val by the step value.
5. Add a condition to check if the value of the counter is equal to or greater than the end value of the object. If it is use the raise StopIteration to end the iteration
6. If the count can continue, return the current counter value.

```
class Counter:
    def __init__(self, start,end,step):
        self.val = start-step
        self.end = end
        self.step = step
    def __iter__(self):
        return self
    def __iter__(self):
        self.val = self.val + self.step
        if self.val >= self.end:
            raise StopIteration
        return self.val

count1 = Counter(1,10,3)
counter1 = iter(count1)
for num in counter1:
    print(num)
```

Output Results :

The provided Python code defines a class called Counter, which is intended to create an iterable sequence of numbers within a specified range. Here's an explanation of the code:

1. class Counter:: This line defines a class named Counter.

2. def __init__(self, start, end, step):: This is the constructor method for the Counter class. It initializes the counter with the starting value (start), the ending value (end), and the step value (step).

a. self: This parameter represents the instance of the class.

b. start: This parameter represents the starting value of the counter.

c. end: This parameter represents the ending value of the counter.

d. step: This parameter represents the step value, which determines the increment between consecutive numbers in the sequence.

     Inside the constructor (__init__) method:

e. self.val = start - step: This line initializes the val attribute to a value just before the starting value, subtracting the step. This ensures that the first iteration starts from the start value.

f. self.end = end: This line sets the end attribute to the provided end parameter.

g. self.step = step: This line sets the step attribute to the provided step parameter.

3. def __iter__(self):: This is a special method that makes the Counter class iterable.

       Inside the __iter__ method:

a. return self: This line returns the instance itself as an iterable.

4. def __next__(self):: This is another special method that defines the behavior of iterating over the Counter object.

       Inside the __next__ method:

a. self.val = self.val + self.step: This line increments the val attribute by the step value.

b. if self.val >= self.end:: This line checks if the val attribute has reached or exceeded the end value.

c. If it has, the method raises a StopIteration exception, indicating the end of the iteration.

d. return self.val: This line returns the current value of val for the next iteration.

5. count1 = Counter(1, 10, 3): This line creates an instance of the Counter class named count1 with a starting value of 1, an ending value of 10, and a step of 3.

6. counter1 = iter(count1): This line calls the iter function on the count1 object to obtain an iterator (counter1) for the Counter instance.

7. for num in counter1:: This line starts a for loop that iterates over the counter1 iterator.

   Inside the loop:

a. print(num): This line prints the current value of num, which is the value generated by the Counter object during each iteration.

The code demonstrates how to create a custom iterable class (Counter) that generates a sequence of numbers within a specified range with a given step size. In this example, it generates numbers from 1 to 10 with a step of 3 and prints them using a for loop.

Exercise Race car class

This exercise will use the class to create several different instances of racecars. Each will have a different name, fuel capacity and engine size. These differences will be used by the drive() method to calculate the distance traveled, and the fuel left. Car speed is determined by the engine size, the larger the number for the engine size the more fuel will be consumed, but it will also cover more distance.

1. Setup the Racecar class. Use the parameters of name, fuel and engine. Create a speed which is based on the engine multiplied by 3. Set the starting distance to 0 for all.

2. In the drive method, the racecar instance gets a value for mileage which will represent the amount of fuel burned each lap. This is an argument from the drive() method.

3. Assign a new value to the fuel, subtracting the mileage and the car engine size.

4. Add a condition to check if the car is out of fuel, if it is then print that the car is out of fuel and the distance that was traveled.

5. If it's not out of fuel, it can still add to the distance. Calculate the new distance by adding the value of the car speed to the distance.

6. Provide the lap feedback within the terminal with the car name, the current distance and the fuel left for each instance of the racecar.

7. Setup a while loop in the global main code area. Set the lap to start at 0

8. Create 3 race cars, using the Racecar class. Use different names, amounts of fuel and engine sizes.

9. Within the while loop, increment the lap, and output the current lap into the terminal with print.

10. Invoke the drive() method for each of the cars.

11. The output result will show the race

```
class Racecar:
    def __init__(main,name,fuel,engine):
        main.name = name
```

```python
        main.fuel = fuel
        main.speed = engine * 3
        main.engine =  engine
        main.distance = 0
    def drive(car,mileage):
        car.fuel = car.fuel - mileage -
car.engine
        if car.fuel > 0:
            car.distance = car.distance +
car.speed
            print(f'({car.name})Distance :
{car.distance} Fuel Left : {car.fuel}')
        else :
            car.fuel = 0
            print(f'({car.name} Ran out of
Gas at {car.distance}')
lap = 0
car1 = Racecar('Civic',50,4)
car2 = Racecar('Corvette',65,10)
car3 = Racecar('Mustang',70,7)
while lap < 5:
    lap = lap + 1
    print(f'Lap # {lap}')
    car1.drive(4)
    car2.drive(10)
    car3.drive(8)
```

Output result :
Lap # 1
(Civic)Distance : 12 Fuel Left : 42
(Corvette)Distance : 30 Fuel Left : 45
(Mustang)Distance : 21 Fuel Left : 55
Lap # 2
(Civic)Distance : 24 Fuel Left : 34
(Corvette)Distance : 60 Fuel Left : 25
(Mustang)Distance : 42 Fuel Left : 40

Lap # 3
(Civic)Distance : 36 Fuel Left : 26
(Corvette)Distance : 90 Fuel Left : 5
(Mustang)Distance : 63 Fuel Left : 25
Lap # 4
(Civic)Distance : 48 Fuel Left : 18
(Corvette Ran out of Gas at 90
(Mustang)Distance : 84 Fuel Left : 10
Lap # 5
(Civic)Distance : 60 Fuel Left : 10
(Corvette Ran out of Gas at 90
(Mustang Ran out of Gas at 84

The provided Python code defines a class called Racecar
that simulates a racecar's behavior, including tracking its
name, fuel, speed, engine power, distance traveled, and the
ability to drive. Here's an explanation of the code:

1. class Racecar:: This line defines a class named Racecar.

2. def __init__(self, name, fuel, engine):: This is the
   constructor method for the Racecar class. It initializes the
   racecar with the following attributes:

a. self: This parameter represents the instance of the class.

b. name: This parameter represents the name of the racecar.

c. fuel: This parameter represents the initial fuel level of the
   racecar.

d. engine: This parameter represents the power of the car's
   engine.

   Inside the constructor (__init__) method:

e. self.name = name: This line sets the name attribute to the
   provided name parameter.

f. self.fuel = fuel: This line sets the fuel attribute to the provided fuel parameter.

g. self.speed = engine * 3: This line calculates the racecar's speed based on the engine power and sets it as the speed attribute.

h. self.engine = engine: This line sets the engine attribute to the provided engine parameter.

i. self.distance = 0: This line initializes the distance attribute to 0, representing the initial distance traveled.

3. def drive(self, mileage):: This method simulates driving the racecar by taking the following parameters:

a. self: This parameter represents the instance of the class.

b. mileage: This parameter represents the distance the racecar will attempt to drive.

   Inside the drive method:

c. self.fuel = self.fuel - mileage - self.engine: This line calculates the remaining fuel after driving a certain distance and accounting for engine power.

   If there is still fuel left:

d. self.distance = self.distance + self.speed: This line updates the distance attribute based on the racecar's speed.

e. It then prints the racecar's name, distance traveled, and remaining fuel.

   If the fuel runs out:

f. The method sets self.fuel to 0 and prints a message indicating that the racecar has run out of gas.

4. lap = 0: This line initializes a variable lap to 0, which will be used to keep track of the laps in the race.

5. Creating Racecar Objects:

a. car1, car2, and car3 are instances of the Racecar class with different characteristics.

6. while lap < 5:: This line starts a while loop that runs for 5 laps.

   Inside the loop:

a. lap = lap + 1: This line increments the lap count.

b. print(f'Lap # {lap}'): This line prints the lap number.

c. Then, for each lap, the drive method is called for each racecar (car1, car2, and car3) with different mileage values to simulate their movement on the track.

The code simulates a race involving three different racecars (car1, car2, and car3) by updating their distances and fuel levels for each lap. The output includes lap numbers, distances traveled, and fuel levels.

Classes are an important part of object-oriented programming. Use of classes creates better structured code, which is easier to manage on larger scale applications. When planning applications, classes are an integral part of the applications planning and development process, which can be used to organize code in logic formats. Selecting to use a class is also determined by the needs of the data structure, and how it is to be organized. In the following chapter we will introduce modules, which much like functions, classes are used to group and organize code in a more structured manner.

Chapter 5 Python modules

Python Modules are files that contain Python code that can be easily brought into other files that can then use the code. Modules provide a way to break down larger applications into smaller more manageable files. Benefit of modules is that they can be plugged into other files, which allows for rapid development of applications. They help keep code organized, which makes it easier to work with to update and scale when needed. You can think of modules like a code library, that can be included into the current code when needed. Prebuilt set of functions that can be grouped so it's easier to use when needed.

Python built in Methods

Python has a number of built-in functions, they get loaded automatically when the Python shell starts. They are always available such as print() and input() and others listed below. Python has built in methods that can be used within the code, they are already defined and can be used to perform various tasks. These built in methods save time for developers. They are a set of commonly used programming methods.

A full list of built in functions is available at
https://docs.python.org/3/library/functions.html

To execute code in string format, use the exec() method, which will parse the string value and execute the code. The output for the below will be the print() of the string contained within.

```
code = 'print("Laurence Svekis")'
```

```
exec(code)
```

Filter method calls a function which returns a boolean for each item contained within an iterable object. The filter will return an iterable object, which can then be iterated through the items.

Exercise to get even numbers from a list

To demonstrate how the filter works, using a list of numbers the filter can be used to select and return only the ones that match the condition. The condition is set up to return a boolean value.

1. Create a list of values, include different odd and even numbers

2. Create a function to check the value of the argument, returning true for values without a remainder and false for values that have a remainder.

3. Using filter() to create a new iterable object of just the values that are even.

4. Using a for, iterate through all the values and print them to the terminal

```
vals = [1,83,36,944,21,2,54,37,100]
def checkEven(v):
    if v%2 == 0:
        return True
    else:
        return False
```

```
res = filter(checkEven,vals)
for num in res:
    print(num)
```

The provided Python code uses the filter function to filter a list of numbers vals and retrieve only the even numbers. Here's an explanation of the code:

1. vals = [1, 83, 36, 944, 21, 2, 54, 37, 100]: This line initializes a list called vals containing a sequence of numbers.

2. def checkEven(v):: This line defines a function named checkEven that takes a single argument v, which represents a value from the vals list.

3. Inside the checkEven function:

a. if v % 2 == 0:: This line checks if the value v is even by performing the modulo operation (%) with 2. If the result is 0, it means the number is even.

b. return True: If the number is even, the function returns True.

c. else:: If the number is not even:

d. return False: The function returns False.

4. res = filter(checkEven, vals): This line uses the filter function to filter the values in the vals list based on the checkEven function. The filter function returns an iterator containing only the values from vals for which checkEven returns True. These values are stored in the res variable.

5. for num in res:: This line iterates over the values in the res iterator, which contains only the even numbers.

6. print(num): Inside the loop, each even number is printed.

In summary, the code defines a function checkEven to determine if a number is even. It then uses the filter function to filter the values in the vals list, retaining only the even numbers. Finally, it iterates through the filtered values and prints each even number.

Each variable is an object in Python, and they each get assigned a unique identity which remains constant. The ids will change once a new instance of the code is executed, but while its executing will remain the same. You can try this with the code below, which will produce 3 numeric values in the output, the first and third one should be the same as its referring to the same value both with the string and the variable assigned the same value of the string.

```
val = 'Hello'
val1 = 'Hello World'
print(id(val))
print(id(val1))
print(id('Hello'))
```

Output
140676890827376
140676892396592
140676890827376

The int() method can be used to convert a string into an integer, if no value is in the arguments then a value of 0 will be returned. If the argument contains a string that cannot be converted into an integer an error will be shown.

```
val = '5'
print(type(val))
val1 = int('5')
print(type(val1))
val2 = int()
print(val2)
```

Output for the above code
<class 'str'>
<class 'int'>
0

To convert a value to a string, use the str() method.

```
val1 = 5
val2 = str(val1)
print(type(val1))
print(type(val2))
```

Output :
<class 'int'>
<class 'str'>

This Python code demonstrates the conversion of a numerical value val1 into a string representation val2. Here's an explanation of each line:

1. val1 = 5: This line assigns the integer value 5 to the variable val1. val1 is now an integer.

2. val2 = str(val1): This line converts the integer val1 into a string using the str() function and assigns the result to the variable val2. After this line, val2 contains the string representation of the integer 5.

3. print(type(val1)): This line prints the data type of the variable val1 using the type() function. Since val1 was initially assigned an integer value, it will print <class 'int'>, indicating that val1 is of type integer.

4. print(type(val2)): This line prints the data type of the variable val2 using the type() function. After the conversion, val2 contains a string, so it will print <class 'str'>, indicating that val2 is of type string.

In summary, this code demonstrates how to convert an integer (val1) into a string (val2) and verifies the data types before and after the conversion using the type() function.

Input() method will return a string value of the input line once the code is executed. It provides a way to intake a value as a string to use within code. The below code will produce a string of whatever value is typed into the terminal.

```
val = input('Enter your name')
print(val)
```

The iter() method returns an iterator object from data. The below code will convert a list into an iterable object.

```
vals1 = [1,83,36,944,21,2,54,37,100]
vals2 = iter(vals1)
print(next(vals2))
```

The len() method can be used to get the count of items in an object like a list. Below code will return the value of 9, which is the number of items in the list.

```
vals1 = [1,83,36,944,21,2,54,37,100]
print(len(vals1))
```

The map() method can be used to return a new iterable object, with the returned results of the updated item value.

Exercise to double all the list values

Similar to what the filter does, the map() returns an updated value of an item as it goes through all the items in the iterable.

1. Create a list of values

2. Create a function which gets one argument, that it adds to itself to double the value and return it.

3. Using map() create a new variable with the results from the doubler function.

4. Using the for in, iterate through all the items in the new iterable object.

```
vals1 = [1,83,36,944,21,2,54,37,100]
def doubler(val):
    return val + val
vals2 = map(doubler,vals1)
for v in vals2:
    print(v)
```

The provided Python code uses the map function to apply the doubler function to each element in the vals1 list and then prints the results. Here's an explanation of the code:

1. vals1 = [1, 83, 36, 944, 21, 2, 54, 37, 100]: This line initializes a list called vals1 containing a sequence of numbers.
2. def doubler(val):: This line defines a function named doubler that takes a single argument val.
3. Inside the doubler function:
a. return val + val: This line doubles the value val by adding it to itself and returns the result.
4. vals2 = map(doubler, vals1): This line uses the map function to apply the doubler function to each element in the vals1 list. The map function returns an iterator containing the results of applying doubler to each element. These results are stored in the vals2 variable.
5. for v in vals2:: This line starts a loop that iterates over the elements of the vals2 iterator.
6. print(v): Inside the loop, each doubled value is printed.

   Here's how the code works:
- The map function applies the doubler function to each element of the vals1 list, resulting in a new iterator (vals2) where each element is doubled.
- The for loop then iterates through the elements in vals2 and prints each doubled value.

   For example, if vals1 contains [1, 83, 36], the code will print:
   2
   166

Each original value in vals1 has been doubled, and those doubled values are printed in the same order.

The reversed() method will return an iterable object which is the reversed order of items from the original.

```
vals1 = [1,5,8,15,22,29,37,40,46]
vals2 = reversed(vals1)
for val in vals2:
    print(val)
```

The min() method returns the lowest value item from the data object. The max() will return the highest value item from the list.

```
vals1 = [1,5,8,15,22,29,37,40,46]
print(min(vals1))
print(max(vals1))
```

Result will be
1
46

The round() method can be used to round the value of the argument to the nearest full number.

```
val1 = 4.6
val2 = 4.1
val3 = 4.5
print(round(val1))
print(round(val2))
print(round(val3))
```

Result output will be
5
4

4

The sum() method can be used to return a total of all the integers contained within an iterable object.

```
vals1 = [1,5,8,15,22,29,37,40,46]
print(sum(vals1))
```

output:
203

The sorted() method can be used to sort values contained within an iterable object. If the values are integers it will sort numerically with the lowest first by default, and if they are strings it will use the first character and then moving to the following characters in order to sort alphabetically, it will sort by default ascending. To sort in reverse order as descending values, the reverse flag in the argument can be set to True.

```
vals1 = [15,22,29,1,5,8,233,37,40,46]
valAsc = sorted(vals1)
valDec = sorted(vals1,reverse = True)
print(valAsc)
print(valDec)

word1 = 'Laurence'
vals2 = [char for char in word1]
vals3 = sorted(vals2)
vals4 = sorted(vals2,reverse = True)
print(vals2)
print(vals3)
print(vals4)

vals5 = ['ab','ac','aa','ca']
print(sorted(vals5))
```

The provided Python code demonstrates the use of the sorted() function to sort lists and strings in both ascending and descending order. Here's an explanation of the code:

For lists:
- vals1 = [15, 22, 29, 1, 5, 8, 233, 37, 40, 46]: This line initializes a list called vals1 containing a sequence of integers.
- valAsc = sorted(vals1): This line sorts the vals1 list in ascending order and assigns the result to the valAsc variable.
- valDec = sorted(vals1, reverse=True): This line sorts the vals1 list in descending order by specifying reverse=True and assigns the result to the valDec variable.
- print(valAsc): This line prints the valAsc list, which is sorted in ascending order.
- print(valDec): This line prints the valDec list, which is sorted in descending order.

For strings:
- word1 = 'Laurence': This line initializes a string called word1.
- vals2 = [char for char in word1]: This line creates a list vals2 containing each character from the word1 string.

- vals3 = sorted(vals2): This line sorts the vals2 list (characters from the string) in ascending order and assigns the result to the vals3 variable.
- vals4 = sorted(vals2, reverse=True): This line sorts the vals2 list in descending order and assigns the result to the vals4 variable.
- print(vals2): This line prints the original list vals2, which contains characters from the string.
- print(vals3): This line prints the vals3 list, which is sorted in ascending order.
- print(vals4): This line prints the vals4 list, which is sorted in descending order.

  For the list vals5:
- vals5 = ['ab', 'ac', 'aa', 'ca']: This line initializes a list called vals5 containing strings.
- print(sorted(vals5)): This line sorts the vals5 list in ascending order and prints the result.

  Here's what the code will print:
  ```
  [1, 5, 8, 15, 22, 29, 37, 40, 46, 233]
  [233, 46, 40, 37, 29, 22, 15, 8, 5, 1]
  ['L', 'a', 'u', 'r', 'e', 'n', 'c', 'e']
  ['L', 'a', 'c', 'c', 'e', 'e', 'n', 'r', 'u']
  ['aa', 'ab', 'ac', 'ca']
  ```
- valAsc contains the sorted list in ascending order.
- valDec contains the sorted list in descending order.

- vals3 contains the characters of the string sorted in ascending order.
- vals4 contains the characters of the string sorted in descending order.
- sorted(vals5) sorts the list of strings in ascending order.

Python Modules

You can use functions and data from other python files in your main file. Modules in Python allow you to import functionality referencing the module to bring the functionality into another file. You can name the module whatever you want, as long as the file extension is .py.

Creating a module is done by creating a Python file. There does not need to be anything specific about the file, it can contain functions, classes, variables which can then be used within the receiving file. Python uses the import statement to bring code in from another file, you can also specify specific variables to bring in from other files.

Exercise create a simple module

This exercise will be to create a one simple function module, that can be imported and used within a second file.

1. Create a new file in the same directory as your main file. Create a function within that file that has two arguments, and returns the added values back.

2. Use the keyword import and the file name without the extension.

3. To invoke the function, use the file name, with a period separating the function name with the arguments.

app5.py
```
import data1
print(data1.adder(3,5))
```

data1.py
```
def adder(a,b):
    return a+b
```

Output result ;
8

4-1 Files in Editor import from other file

4-2 Second file in the editor

Renaming the module

To set an alternative name as an alias for the file you can use the as keyword. This will provide a way to set a new reference name. From the above code, use the import with as to set a new reference name

```
import data1 as val
print(val.adder(3,5))
```

You can add more functions to the module source file, and they can then be referenced using the same function names that are in the module.

```
def adder(a,b):
    return a+b
def mults(a,b):
    return a*b
```

```
import data1 as val
print(val.adder(3,5))
print(val.mults(3,5))
```

Just as we can reference the functions, variables can also be referenced using the module. In the below example a variable with name1 contains a string value. Its added to the module and now can be accessed within the other file.

```
def adder(a,b):
    return a+b
name1 = 'Laurence Svekis'
```

```
import data1 as val
print(val.name1);
```

You can import multiple modules, the modules do need to be defined which can be done using the import keyword and the file name without the extension. You can also import specific objects from the module, but using the from keyword. The form specifies which file module, and the import specificity which object to import, keeping the object name. Below code sample will import the name1 value as name1, which can then be used in the code. Only the specified object will be imported, with no need to prefix it with the module.

```
from data2 import name1
print(name1);
```

```
data2.py
```

```
name1 = 'John Smith'
name2 = 'Laurence Svekis'
name3 = 'Jane Doe'
```

To import all the objects contained within the module directly into the main code, you can use the wildcard *.

```
from data2 import *
print(name1);
print(name2);
print(name3);
```

Output result :
John Smith
Laurence Svekis
Jane Doe

Exercise : Module data greeter

Greeting function using data from two different modules to output a welcome message into the terminal.

1. Create a Python file with the name data.py, in the file create a dictionary with the name myName and values for the properties of first, last and status. Use your name in the values.

2. Create a Python file with the name mod.py, create a function expecting two arguments. The first and last, create a string and assign the value of first + last to the string named fullName. Using print() create a welcome message using the fullName.

3. Within the mod.py module file, create a dictionary with the same structure as the data.py file, change the property values.

4. Create a python file, import all the objects from mod

5. Import the objects from data3 using an alias of person.

6. Create two statements that invoke the welcome function, and use the first and last names from both sources as the arguments.

```
app.py
from mod import *
import data as person
welcome(myName["first"],myName["last"])
```

```
welcome(person.myName["first"],person.myNam
e["last"])

mod.py
def welcome(first,last):
    fullName = first + " " + last
    print("Welcome to my page, " + fullName)
myName = {
    "first" : "John",
    "last" : "Smith",
    "status" : True
}

data.py
myName = {
    "first" : "Laurence",
    "last" : "Svekis",
    "status" : True
}
```

The provided code consists of three separate Python files: app.py, mod.py, and data.py. Here's an explanation of how these files work together:

app.py:
- This is the main Python script that imports functions and data from the other two files.
- It imports everything (*) from the mod module and imports the myName dictionary from the data module as person.myName.
- It calls the welcome function from the mod module, passing in the values of myName["first"] and myName["last"] (from the mod module) as arguments.

- It also calls the welcome function again, this time passing in the values of person.myName["first"] and person.myName["last"] (from the data module) as arguments.

mod.py:
- This module defines a welcome function that takes first and last as arguments.

- Inside the welcome function, it constructs the fullName by concatenating first and last.

- It then prints a welcome message that includes the fullName.

data.py:
- This module defines a myName dictionary that contains information about a person, including their first name, last name, and status.

When you run app.py, it first imports the functions and data from the other two modules. Then, it calls the welcome function from the mod module twice:

- The first call uses the myName dictionary from the mod module, which contains the values for "John" and "Smith."

- The second call uses the myName dictionary from the data module, which contains the values for "Laurence" and "Svekis."

As a result, you'll see two welcome messages printed, one for each set of first and last values, using data from different modules.

Here's what the output might look like when you run app.py:
Welcome to my page, John Smith
Welcome to my page, Laurence Svekis
In summary, app.py acts as the main script that imports and utilizes functions and data from mod.py and data.py. The specific values passed to the welcome function depend on which module's myName dictionary is used.

How to Import Built-in Modules Python

Just as we saw with built-in functions there are a number of built-in modules. Just as when we create modules, they are Python files with functions built-in modules can also be imported and used within Python code. These libraries are bundled with Python distributions, and available to be imported as needed. Unlike the built-in functions that get loaded automatically, these modules if needed will need to be imported.

Using the built-in modules can save development time, as they provide access to commonly needed functionality and are extremely useful when developing code.

There are a lot of really useful modules, a complete module index can be viewed at https://docs.python.org/3/py-modindex.html

The datetime built in module

The datetime built-in module, is a standard module that you can use to get date values. The datetime is the main function within the datetime module. To import and use the datetime you can import datetime, or use the from datetime import datetime to bring in only the datetime object. This saves writing datetime.datetime twice to use the object.

To get the current timestamp there is a method now(). The now() method returns property with values and methods. The current day date is a property, as well as the month and year. To return the index value of the current day there is a method named weekday(), the result is a numeric value for the day, as it is starting at zero from Monday. For example datetime.now().weekday() would return 3 on a Thursday, where Monday would be 0 and the rest of the days increment accordingly. This can be used as an index value for a list, as lists start with zero. Below code gets the day, month, and year.

```
from datetime import datetime
today = datetime.now()
print(today)
print(today.day)
print(today.month)
print(today.year)
print(today.weekday())
```

Output Result
2024-01-05 18:32:18.503977
5
1
2024
3

Exercise Show the day name

This exercise will use the day names in a list, starting with Monday and then use the weekday() method to get the index value of the day to show.

1. import the datetime module

2. Set the current date to a variable named today

3. Create a list of names of the days, starting with Mon, Tues.....

4. Print the current day name into the terminal

```
from datetime import datetime
today = datetime.now()
days =
["Mon","Tues","Wed","Thurs","Fri","Sat","Su
n"]
print(days[today.weekday()])
```

Output for Thursday, please note it will vary depending on the current day.
Thurs

The provided Python code utilizes the datetime module to determine the day of the week for the current date. Here's an explanation of how the code works:

1. from datetime import datetime: This line imports the datetime class from the datetime module. The datetime class allows you to work with date and time objects.

2. today = datetime.now(): This line creates a datetime object named today representing the current date and time. The datetime.now() function is used to obtain the current date and time.

3. days = ["Mon", "Tues", "Wed", "Thurs", "Fri", "Sat", "Sun"]: This line defines a list called days that contains abbreviated names for the days of the week, starting with Monday ("Mon") and ending with Sunday ("Sun").

4. print(days[today.weekday()]): This line prints the name of the day of the week corresponding to the current date. Here's how it works:

a. today.weekday() returns an integer representing the day of the week, where Monday is 0, Tuesday is 1, and so on, up to Sunday being 6.

b. The today.weekday() value is used as an index to access the corresponding day abbreviation from the days list.

c. The result is printed to the console.

For example, if you run this code on a Tuesday, it will output:
Tues
It dynamically determines the day of the week based on the current date and time and prints the corresponding abbreviation.

The datetime can also be used to create and set a specific date to a date object. Within the parenthesis of the datetime() method add a comma separated value for three parameters, year, month, day.

```
from datetime import datetime
today = datetime(2023,1,5)
print(today)
```

Exercise Show day of the week part 2

Using the code from the previous exercise, determine and output the result for what day of the week New year's day falls on each year starting in 2020 and ending 2029.

1. import the datetime and use the days list from previous exercise

2. Set a variable named startYear to 2020

3. Use while to loop until the startYear reaches 2030

4. Set the first day date object

5. create an output using the startYear and the index value of days list item, from the weekday() method.

6. Print the output and increment startYear to move to the following year.

```
from datetime import datetime
days =
["Mon","Tues","Wed","Thurs","Fri","Sat","Su
n"]
startYear = 2020
while(startYear  < 2030):
    first = datetime(startYear,1,1)
    output = 'In {} new years day is on a
{}'.format(startYear,days[first.weekday()])
```

```
    print(output )
    startYear+=1
```

Expected output :
In 2020 new years day is on a Wed
In 2021 new years day is on a Fri
In 2022 new years day is on a Sat
In 2023 new years day is on a Sun
In 2024 new years day is on a Mon
In 2025 new years day is on a Wed
In 2026 new years day is on a Thurs
In 2027 new years day is on a Fri
In 2028 new years day is on a Sat
In 2029 new years day is on a Mon

Python Built-in OS module

The OS module can be used to perform typical system tasks, including functions for creating folders and getting contents. To see the current directory use the os, and the method getcwd(). To make a new folder use the mkdir() with the argument for the folder name.

```
import os
print(os.getcwd())
os.mkdir("tester")
```

Python Built-in Math Module

Math module provides methods for working with numbers, and use of typical math functions. There are various property values like PI, and methods to round down to the floor or up to the next full number with ceil. There is also the power of and square root.

```python
import math
val = 5.5
print(math.pi)
print(math.ceil(val))
print(math.floor(val))
print(math.pow(3,3))
print(math.sqrt(100))
```

The provided Python code demonstrates the usage of the math module to perform various mathematical operations. Here's an explanation of each line of code:

1. import math: This line imports the math module, which provides access to a wide range of mathematical functions and constants.

2. val = 5.5: This line assigns the value 5.5 to the variable val, which is used for performing mathematical operations in the subsequent code.

3. print(math.pi): This line prints the mathematical constant π (pi), which is approximately equal to 3.141592653589793. The math.pi constant is provided by the math module.

4. print(math.ceil(val)): This line uses the math.ceil() function to round the value of val up to the nearest integer. In this

case, 5.5 is rounded up to 6. The math.ceil() function always rounds up.

5. print(math.floor(val)): This line uses the math.floor() function to round the value of val down to the nearest integer. In this case, 5.5 is rounded down to 5. The math.floor() function always rounds down.

6. print(math.pow(3, 3)): This line calculates and prints the result of raising 3 to the power of 3. It uses the math.pow() function, where the first argument is the base (3 in this case) and the second argument is the exponent (3 in this case). The result is 27.

7. print(math.sqrt(100)): This line calculates and prints the square root of 100 using the math.sqrt() function. The square root of 100 is 10.0.

When you run this code, you'll get the following output:
```
3.141592653589793
6
5
27.0
10.0
```
It demonstrates the usage of several mathematical functions and constants provided by the math module in Python.

The Python built-in statistics module

The statistics module contains methods to get statistics from data.

```
import statistics
val = [15,22,29,1,5,8,233,37,40,46]
print(statistics.mean(val))
print(statistics.median(val))
print(statistics.mode(val))
```

Output result :

43.6
25.5
15

The time module in Python

The time module provides various time related functionality. The time sleep() method takes an argument that is used as the number of seconds to suspend the execution. This is useful for scripts that need counting and pausing of execution for a preset period. The below code will create a timer that outputs the next number after a 1 second pause, counting until 10

```
import time
val = 0
while val < 11:
    val+=1
    print(val)
    time.sleep(1)
```

Output result
1
2
...
9
10

Create a countdown timer

Within the terminal enter a number in seconds of how long
you want the countdown to count. The countdown will
continue until it reaches 0. Using the datetime, time format
can be output using the timedelta() method.

1. Import the time and datetime modules
2. Create a start function that will get the input from the user
   as to how many seconds the countdown should run.
3. Within the start function check if the input is numeric, if it
   is send the seconds as an integer to a new function named
   countdown, if the input was not numeric, provide
   feedback to the user
4. Create a function named countdown that will loop and
   decrease the value of the remaining seconds. The number
   of total seconds should be set in the function argument and
   passed in from the start function.

5. Create a string output value using format to structure it as minutes and seconds. Use the datetime timedelta() to convert the seconds to a string output formatted in a time.

6. Create the output message for the user stating the amount of time left.

7. Using the time module import the sleep method slowing the output with a 1 second delay

8. Subtract from the total seconds

9. Once the while loop completes print the time is up blast off message and invoke the start function again

10. Add the start() function to launch the input and countdown.

```python
import time
import datetime

def countdown(t):
    while t:
        counter =
datetime.timedelta(seconds=t)
        output = "Time Left is
{}".format(counter)
        print(output)
        time.sleep(1)
        t -= 1
    print("Blast OFF!!!")
    start()
def start():
```

```
    t = input("Enter the number of seconds :
")
    if t.isnumeric() :
        countdown(int(t))
    else:
        print("Please enter a number ")
start()
```

The expected output result :
Enter the number of seconds : 4
Time Left is 00:04
Time Left is 00:03
Time Left is 00:02
Time Left is 00:01
Blast OFF!!!

The provided Python code creates a countdown timer using the time and datetime modules. Here's an explanation of each part of the code:

1. import time: This line imports the time module, which provides various time-related functions, including the sleep function used for introducing delays.

2. import datetime: This line imports the datetime module, which provides classes and functions for working with dates and times.

3. def countdown(t): This defines a function named countdown that takes an argument t, which represents the countdown time in seconds.

   Inside the function:

a. It enters a while loop that runs as long as t is greater than 0.

b. Inside the loop, it creates a counter using datetime.timedelta(seconds=t). This counter represents the remaining time in seconds and is used for formatting the countdown message.

c. It formats and prints the countdown message, displaying the remaining time in seconds.

d. It uses time.sleep(1) to introduce a one-second delay in each iteration, effectively creating a one-second interval between countdown updates.

e. It decrements t by 1 in each iteration to update the countdown.

f. Once the countdown reaches 0, it prints "Blast OFF!!!" to indicate the end of the countdown.

4. def start(): This defines a function named start responsible for getting the user's input for the countdown duration.

   Inside the function:

a. It prompts the user to enter the number of seconds for the countdown using input().

b. It checks if the input value t is numeric using t.isnumeric().

c. If the input is numeric, it calls the countdown function, passing the integer value of t as the countdown duration.

d. If the input is not numeric, it prints "Please enter a number."

5. start(): This line of code calls the start function to initiate the countdown timer.

When you run this code, it will prompt you to enter the number of seconds for the countdown. After entering the duration, it will start the countdown and display the remaining time in seconds with a one-second interval between updates. Once the countdown reaches 0, it will print "Blast OFF!!!" and then allow you to start another countdown by calling start() again.

Python built in Random Module

Python has a random module which can be used to generate random variables. This is a very useful module as it can generate a random number, also be used to select and randomize list values. The randint() requires two arguments, the first is the min number and the second is the max number of the random number to be generated. The results will return a random number between and including the minimum and the maximum numbers. The below code example will generate 10 random numbers, between 1 and 10 including the 1 and 10

```
import random
i = 0
while i < 10:
    ran = random.randint(1,10)
    print(ran)
    i+=1
```

Output result
10
7
8
9

The provided Python code uses the random module to generate and print 10 random integers between 1 and 10. Here's an explanation of each part of the code:

1. import random: This line imports the random module, which provides functions for generating random numbers.

2. i = 0: This line initializes a variable i to 0. It is used to control the loop and ensure that it runs exactly 10 times.

3. while i < 10:: This line starts a while loop that continues to execute as long as the value of i is less than 10.

   Inside the loop:

a. ran = random.randint(1, 10): This line generates a random integer using the randint function from the random module. The function takes two arguments: the lower bound (1 in this case) and the upper bound (10 in this case), inclusive. It returns a random integer between 1 and 10 (including both 1 and 10) and assigns it to the variable ran.

b. print(ran): This line prints the randomly generated integer.

c. i += 1: This line increments the value of i by 1 in each iteration, ensuring that the loop will eventually exit after 10 iterations.

In summary, this code generates 10 random integers between 1 and 10 and prints each of them in sequence. The while loop controls the repetition of this process until it has been executed 10 times.

To generate random numbers not including the numbers in the argument, and only between the two the randrange() method can be used.

```
import random
i = 0
while i < 10:
    ran = random.randrange(1,10)
    print(ran)
    i+=1
```

Random can also be used on lists, to either make a random selection from a list or to shuffle the entire list in place changing the index values for the items.

```
import random
people = ['Laurence','Sam','Jane']
i = 0
while i < 5:
    ran = random.choice(people)
    print(ran)
    i+=1
print(people)
random.shuffle(people)
print(people)
```

Output result :
Laurence
Laurence
Sam
Laurence
Sam
['Laurence', 'Sam', 'Jane']
['Sam', 'Laurence', 'Jane']

Exercise Dice game in Python

This exercise will use the random module to generate random values. The values are going to be a number from 1 - 6 and represent a simulation of what can be rolled with dice. The overall score will be tracked across the rounds, the player can control how many rounds are played. Each round the random values for both the player and computer will be compared. The highest value wins, and will get scored for as the winner of the round.

1. import the random module

2. Set variables for the minimum and max values for the roll.

3. Set starting score values for the computer and for the player of 0

4. Setup a global value to track the game play, which can be set to true as a starting value. Once it is set to false the game should be ended.

5. Create a function named gamePlay() Within the function bring in the inPlay, and scores from the global values

6. Create a loop to continue until inPlay is no longer True

7. Generate a random value for both the player and computer

8. Print the values to the player in the terminal

9. Apply a condition to check who won, or if it was a tie. Increase the score accordingly. Provide the player feedback of the result.

10. Ask the player to roll again, if the inPlay equal exit breaks out of the loop. If the player presses enter the inPlay will be false and break out of the loop as well.
11. Launch the gamePlay() function
12. Create game over feedback, including the total scores from the gameplay.

```
import random
min = 1
max = 6
computerScore = 0
playerScore = 0
inPlay = True
def gamePlay():
 global inPlay
 global computerScore
 global playerScore
 while inPlay:
    player = random.randint(min,max)
    computer = random.randint(min,max)
    print(f"You Got {player} vs {computer}")
    if(player == computer):
       print("Tie Game")
    elif (player > computer):
       print("Player Wins")
       playerScore += 1
    elif (player < computer):
       print("Computer Wins")
       computerScore += 1
    inPlay = input("Roll Again ? ")
    if inPlay == "exit" :
       break
 gamePlay()
 print("Game Over")
```

```python
print(f"Computer Score : {computerScore } vs Player Score :
{playerScore }")
```

This Python code is a simple dice game that allows a player to roll a virtual die and compete against the computer. Here's an explanation of how the code works:

1. import random: This line imports the random module, which is used to generate random numbers.

2. min = 1 and max = 6: These lines set the minimum and maximum values for the virtual die, simulating a standard six-sided die.

3. computerScore = 0 and playerScore = 0: These lines initialize variables to keep track of the computer's and player's scores.

4. inPlay = True: This variable is used to control the game loop. It is initially set to True to start the game.

5. def gamePlay():: This line defines a function called gamePlay that contains the game logic.

6. global statements: Inside the gamePlay function, there are several global statements. These statements indicate that the variables being referenced within the function are the same as the global variables defined outside the function.

7. while inPlay:: This line starts a while loop that continues as long as the inPlay variable is True, meaning the game is ongoing.

   Inside the loop:

a. player = random.randint(min, max): This line generates a random integer for the player's roll, between 1 and 6, and assigns it to the player variable.

b. computer = random.randint(min, max): This line generates a random integer for the computer's roll, between 1 and 6, and assigns it to the computer variable.

c. print(f"You Got {player} vs {computer}"): This line prints the results of the player's and computer's rolls.

d. The following if statements determine the outcome of each round:

- If the player and computer rolls are equal, it's a tie game.
- If the player's roll is greater, the player wins, and their score is incremented.
- If the computer's roll is greater, the computer wins, and its score is incremented.

e. inPlay = input("Roll Again ? "): This line prompts the player to decide whether to roll the dice again or exit the game. If the player enters "exit," the game loop will break.

8. gamePlay(): This line calls the gamePlay function to start the game.

9. print("Game Over"): This line prints "Game Over" when the game is finished.

10. print(f"Computer Score: {computerScore} vs Player Score: {playerScore}"): This line displays the final scores for the computer and player.

In summary, this code simulates a dice game where the player and the computer take turns rolling a die, and their scores are updated based on the outcome of each roll. The game continues until the player chooses to exit, and the final scores are displayed at the end.

In this section we covered the prebuilt functionality that can be easily brought into your code whether they are pre-built functions or importing of modules. Explore creating your own modules with custom functionality. The great thing about using modules is that you can build your own library over time which will help increase the speed of development of new projects, as you can and should build modules that can be repurposed. In the upcoming section we will be covering Python in action, demonstrating more advanced applications of Python code to build fun projects.

Chapter 6 Projects with Python

In this chapter we are going to demonstrate how to import external file contents. Also how to use JSON data within your Python applications. JSON data is a common data format used within applications. It works across programming languages and provides a structured way to view and manage data.

File handling with Python

Python can be used to open and interact with files. Using the open() method this can be used to open a file, then as the second argument use the mode.

'a' - APPEND - to open and add to a file. It will create a new file if the file does not exist.
'r' = READ - to open and read the contents of the file
'w' = WRITE - to open and write to the file contents
'x' = CREATE a file

The below will create a new file and write the contents into it.

```
temp1 = open('new1.txt','a')
temp1.write('-New Content added-')
temp1.close()
```

To open and read the contents of a file use 'r'

```
temp2 = open('new1.txt','r')
print(temp2.read())
```

To overwrite the contents of a file use the 'w'

```
temp3 = open('new1.txt','w')
temp3.write('This is the new content now')
temp3.close()
```

The output of the above code will be This is the new content now-New Content added- once its run more than once.

The OS module can be used to create and update files and folders.
To rename a file use the code below
import os
```
os.rename( "new1.txt", "new2.txt" )
```

To remove a file use the remove() method from the OS module

```
os.remove('new2.txt')
```

Exercise StoryMaker how to Create a story

This exercise will create a new text file with a unique story from the input values. The code runs and asks 5 questions which the user supplies answers for. The story is then created as a string value which is output in the terminal and also written to a file named story.txt

1. Create several inputs needed for the story. You can customize them.

2. Using the values of the responses to the inputs, create a string from the responses adding supporting text.

3. Print the story to the user

4. Create a file and store the new story into the file.

```python
place = input('Enter a place: ')
name1 = input('Enter a name: ')
name2 = input('Enter a second name: ')
item1 = input('Enter an item: ')
color1 = input('Enter a color: ')

story1 = f'{name1} went to {place} to get a
{color1} {item1}, when {name1} arrived
{name2} already had the {item1}'
print(story1)
storyFile = open('story.txt','w')
storyFile.write(story1)
storyFile.close()
```

Resulting output:
Enter a place: hill
Enter a name: Laurence
Enter a second name: Sam
Enter an item: sandwich
Enter a color: blue
Laurence went to hill to get a blue sandwich, when
Laurence arrived Sam already had the sandwich

This Python code is a simple interactive script that takes
user input to create a short story and then writes that story
to a text file. Here's how the code works:

1. place = input('Enter a place: '): This line prompts the user
   to enter a place (e.g., a city or location), and the input is
   stored in the variable place.

2. name1 = input('Enter a name: '): This line prompts the user
   to enter a name (e.g., a person's name), and the input is
   stored in the variable name1.

3. name2 = input('Enter a second name: '): This line prompts
   the user to enter a second name (e.g., another person's
   name), and the input is stored in the variable name2.

4. item1 = input('Enter an item: '): This line prompts the user
   to enter an item (e.g., an object), and the input is stored in
   the variable item1.

5. color1 = input('Enter a color: '): This line prompts the user
   to enter a color, and the input is stored in the variable
   color1.

6. story1 = f'{name1} went to {place} to get a {color1} {item1}, when {name1} arrived {name2} already had the {item1}': This line creates a short story using f-strings (formatted strings) and combines the user inputs (name1, place, color1, item1, and name2) to form the story.

7. print(story1): This line prints the generated story to the console.

8. storyFile = open('story.txt', 'w'): This line opens a file named "story.txt" in write mode ('w') and assigns it to the storyFile variable. If the file doesn't exist, it will be created. If it already exists, its contents will be overwritten.

9. storyFile.write(story1): This line writes the generated story (story1) to the opened file.

10. storyFile.close(): This line closes the file, ensuring that changes are saved and freeing up system resources associated with the file.

In summary, this code interacts with the user to collect input for a short story. It then creates the story by combining the user's inputs and prints it to the console. Additionally, it writes the story to a text file named "story.txt." If the file already exists, its contents are replaced with the new story.

Exercise guess the secret animal

In this exercise there is a list of animals, one is selected at random as a secret value. The application will give you a hint of what the last letter is, and provide 3 tries to guess the correct animal.

1. Create a list of animals
2. import the random module
3. Create a function that sets up a variable for a guess, has counter to track the guesses and has a boolean inPlay variable
4. Using the random module select a random animal
5. Create a hint for the player selecting the last letter in the animal
6. Using while create a loop until the counter reaches 3 or the player guesses correctly.
7. Ask for an input for the guess, increment the counter
8. If the loop guess is correct, end the gameplay setting the inPlay to True
9. Once the round ends, provide feedback to the player, if they guessed correctly show that as the output.
10. Provide an opportunity to play again.
11. Invoke the game and print the game over once the function is complete.

```
import random
```

```python
animals =
['cat','dog','snake','duck','bear','frog']

def game():
    guess = ''
    inPlay = False
    counter = 0
    correct = random.choice(animals)
    print(f'HINT: it ends with {correct[-
1]}')
    while guess.lower() != correct and
not(inPlay):
        if counter < 3:
            guess = input('Enter an Animal:
')
            counter += 1
        else:
            inPlay = True
    if inPlay:
        print(f'You are out of guesses it
was {correct}.')
    else:
        print(f'You got it, {correct} was
correct.')
    playAgain = input('Would you like to
play again? Y/N? ')
    if playAgain.lower() == 'y':
        game()
game()
print('Game Over')
```

Output result:
HINT: it ends with r
Enter an Animal: cat
Enter an Animal: bear
You got it, bear was correct.

Would you like to play again? Y/N?

This Python code is a simple guessing game where the player has to guess the name of an animal. Here's how the code works:

1. import random: This line imports the random module, which allows the program to generate random numbers and make random choices.
2. animals = ['cat','dog','snake','duck','bear','frog']: This line creates a list called animals that contains several animal names as strings.
3. def game():: This line defines a function called game() where the guessing game logic is implemented.
4. guess = '': This initializes an empty string guess to store the player's guesses.
5. inPlay = False: This initializes a boolean variable inPlay to False, indicating that the game is not yet in progress.
6. counter = 0: This initializes a variable counter to keep track of the number of guesses the player has made.
7. correct = random.choice(animals): This line randomly selects an animal name from the animals list and assigns it to the correct variable. This is the animal the player needs to guess.
8. print(f'HINT: it ends with {correct[-1]}'): This line provides a hint to the player about the last letter of the correct animal's name.

9. The while loop: This loop continues as long as the player's guess is not equal to the correct animal name and the player still has remaining guesses (less than 3).

a. guess = input('Enter an Animal: '): Inside the loop, the player is prompted to enter an animal name, and their input is stored in the guess variable.

b. counter += 1: The counter is incremented to keep track of the number of guesses.

c. If the player enters three incorrect guesses, inPlay is set to True, and the loop exits.

10. After the loop, the code checks whether the game ended because the player guessed the correct animal or ran out of guesses.

a. If inPlay is True, it means the player ran out of guesses, and a message is printed indicating the correct animal.

b. If inPlay is still False, it means the player guessed the correct animal, and a congratulatory message is printed.

1. playAgain = input('Would you like to play again? Y/N? '): The player is asked if they want to play again, and their input is stored in the playAgain variable.

2. If the player enters 'y' (case insensitive), the game() function is called again, allowing them to play another round.

3. The game starts by calling the game() function.

4. Finally, a message, "Game Over," is printed to indicate the end of the game.

In summary, this code creates a simple animal guessing game where the player has to guess an animal's name based on a hint. The player is limited to three guesses per round and can choose to play again after each round.

Exercise Random Password Generator

This exercise will create a random set of 8 characters and return the value to the user. Included is a way to shuffle the letters of a string in the maker() function. This is not necessary for the basic password but will show how you can use a string and randomize the order of the characters.

1. import the random module
2. Create a function that will get a value, and convert it to a list. Using random shuffle the list values and join them back into a string returning a shuffled string order.
3. Create a loop that will add a new character to a string value. Loop for the number of characters in the password using random randint to select a chr() value randomly.
4. Randomize the string characters in the string, and return it as a password.

5. Create a second loop to output 5 variations of the password string

```python
import random

def maker(p):
  temp = list(p)
  random.shuffle(temp)
  return ''.join(temp)

i = 0
password = '';
while i < 8:
    password = password +
chr(random.randint(65,90))
    i+=1

x = 0
while x < 5:
    password = maker(password)
    print(password)
    x+=1
```

Output result :

FJCIATWP
TCWPFAIJ
FWIPTCAJ
PFTWCIAJ
CITWJFPA

This Python code generates random passwords. Here's how it works:

1. import random: This line imports the random module, which is used to generate random numbers and shuffle characters in the password.
2. def maker(p): This is a function called maker that takes a string p as input. It shuffles the characters in the input string and returns the shuffled string.
   - temp = list(p): Converts the input string p into a list of characters.
   - random.shuffle(temp): Shuffles the characters in the list randomly.
   - return ''.join(temp): Converts the shuffled list of characters back into a string and returns it.
3. i = 0, password = '': These lines initialize a counter i and an empty string password.
4. The first while loop (while i < 8) generates an initial password of 8 uppercase letters (A-Z).
   - password = password + chr(random.randint(65,90)): It appends a random uppercase letter (represented by ASCII values 65 to 90) to the password string in each iteration.
5. x = 0: This line initializes another counter x.
6. The second while loop (while x < 5) generates 5 random passwords by repeatedly calling the maker function.
   - password = maker(password): Calls the maker function with the current password string, which shuffles the characters and updates the password variable.

o   print(password): Prints the generated password.

7. After generating and printing five random passwords, the code terminates.

In summary, this code generates random passwords by first creating an initial password with 8 random uppercase letters and then repeatedly shuffling the characters in the password to create additional random passwords. The final passwords are printed to the console.

Exercise Rock Paper Scissors Game

This is a classic version of rock paper, scissors game. Where the player selects one of the choices, and the opponent does the same. The Rock will beat out the scissors, scissors will beat out a paper, and a paper will beat out a rock. There is also a possibility of a tie game if both players select the same item.

1. Import the random module

2. Set both the player and computer scores to 0

3. Create a list of the selectable items rock paper, scissors

4. Set a boolean value variable for game play.

5. Create a function named gamePlay() which will contain the game object

6. Use global to get the global variables

7. Get the player selection, capitalize() the response so that it can be made consistent with the list values

8. Randomly select an item for the computer from the list

9. Provide output feedback on the selections for both the player and the computer.
10. Apply conditions to check for a tie game, if no tie is found then using the else if check for the other win conditions.
11. Depending on the result from the condition update the score of the winner. Output the score to the player and ask to play again.

```python
import random
computerScore = 0
playerScore = 0
arr = ["Rock","Paper","Scissors"]
inPlay = True
def gamePlay():
    global inPlay
    global computerScore
    global playerScore
    while inPlay:
        player = input("Rock Paper or
Scissors ? ").capitalize()
        computer =
random.choice(arr).capitalize()
        print(f"You Selected : {player} vs
Computer Selected : {computer}")
        if player ==  computer :
            print("Tie Game")
        elif player == "Rock":
            if(computer == "Paper"):
                print("You Lose")
                computerScore+=1
            else:
                print("You win")
```

```python
            playerScore += 1
        elif player == "Paper":
            if(computer == "Scissors"):
                print("You Lose")
                computerScore+=1
            else:
                print("You win")
                playerScore += 1
        elif player == "Scissors":
            if(computer == "Rock"):
                print("You Lose")
                computerScore+=1
            else:
                print("You win")
                playerScore += 1
        print(f"You ({playerScore}) vs
Computer({computerScore})")
        inPlay = input("Play Again ? ")
    print("Game Over")
    print(f"Your Score ({playerScore}) vs
Computer({computerScore})")
gamePlay()
```

Output Result :
Rock Paper or Scissors ? rock
You Selected : Rock vs Computer Selected : Scissors
You win
You (1) vs Computer(0)

This Python code is for a simple Rock, Paper, Scissors game where the user plays against the computer. Here's an explanation of how the code works:

1. Import the random module: This code begins by importing the random module, which is used to generate random choices for the computer's moves.

2. Initialize scores and options: The code initializes variables to keep track of the scores for the computer (computerScore) and the player (playerScore). It also creates a list arr containing the three possible choices: "Rock," "Paper," and "Scissors."

3. gamePlay function: The main game logic is defined within the gamePlay function. This function uses global variables to keep track of the game's state and scores.

4. Game Loop: Inside the gamePlay function, there is a while loop that continues until inPlay is set to False. This loop allows the player to keep playing the game until they choose to exit.

5. Player's Move: The player is prompted to enter their choice, which is stored in the player variable. The capitalize() method is used to ensure that the player's choice is in title case (e.g., "Rock" instead of "rock").

6. Computer's Move: The computer's choice is generated randomly using random.choice(arr). This means the computer selects one of the three options from the arr list.

7. Determine the Winner: The code then compares the player's choice and the computer's choice to determine the

winner. The logic considers the rules of the Rock, Paper, Scissors game. The outcomes are printed on the screen.

8. Score Update: The code updates the computerScore and playerScore variables based on the game's outcome and prints the current scores.

9. Play Again: The player is asked if they want to play again. If they enter anything other than "Y" (case insensitive), the inPlay variable is set to False, which exits the game loop.

10. Game Over: After exiting the game loop, the code prints "Game Over" and displays the final scores.

11. Function Invocation: Finally, the gamePlay function is invoked to start the game.

The game continues until the player decides to quit, and the scores are displayed at the end of each game.

JSON module in Python

JSON is a commonly used data format online. The structure is similar to the dictionary, and based on object structure where the data can contain a property key that can return a value. The data is stored as key value pairs, and can also contain lists of values. To make use of a JSON file, Python has the json module.

Below is an example of JSON data. The Data lists 3
questions, each with their own objects of data. JSON
format is a preferred format for data online as it works
easily across programming languages and can be easily
read by a human. The structure data can vary in data
types.

Example of JSON data

```
[{
    "question": "What color is an apple"
    , "answers": ["Blue",  "Purple"]
    , "correct": "Red"
}
 , {
    "question": "What color is Grass"
    , "answers": ["Blue", "Red", "Purple"]
    , "correct": "Green"
}
 , {
    "question": "Is the Sky Blue"
    , "answers": [ "False"]
    , "correct": "True"
}
]
```

Exercise Use JSON data in your Python Code

JSON data files can contain a lot of useful data information,
which can be brought in and used within your code.

1. Create the above data as a file named data.json

2. Use the import to import the json module into the Python code

3. Get the file contents and read them to a variable named data

4. Using the json.loads() method then load the data value as a usable object in Python.

5. Using the square brackets select a question value from the json file and output it into the terminal.

```
import json

file = open('data.json','r')
data = file.read()
json = json.loads(data)
print(json[0]['question'])
```

Output result :
What color is an apple

This Python code is used to read and parse JSON data from a file named 'data.json'. Here's an explanation of how the code works:

1. Import the json module: The code begins by importing the json module, which provides methods for working with JSON data.

2. Open and Read the JSON File: It opens the 'data.json' file in read mode using open('data.json', 'r') and assigns the file object to the file variable.

3. Read JSON Data: The code reads the contents of the file using the file.read() method and assigns the JSON data as a string to the variable data.

4. Parse JSON Data: The json.loads(data) function is used to parse the JSON data stored in the data variable. It converts the JSON string into a Python data structure, which is typically a list or dictionary in this case.

5. Access JSON Data: Once the JSON data is parsed, it is stored in the json variable. The code then accesses the first element of the list (json[0]) and retrieves the value associated with the key 'question' using json[0]['question'].

6. Print the Result: Finally, the code prints the value of the 'question' key from the first element of the JSON data. This will display the question stored in the JSON file.

In summary, this code reads JSON data from a file, parses it, and extracts and prints a specific piece of information (the value associated with the 'question' key in the first element of the JSON data).

Exercise Python JSON quiz

Load JSON data from an external file into your code. The JSON structure is the one used previously where there are a set of questions, which each contain data. Present the questions one at a time to the player, provide the options for the correct answer. Create an input and check if the player got the question correct, score the results of the game.

1. import both the json and random modules

2. Open and read the json file contents, convert to a usable data object.

3. Create a main function for the game. Load the questions from the json object

4. Set the score and counter variables to zero

5. Loop through the questions in the dictionary object. Increment counter by one. Create a list of the answers, append the correct answer to the incorrect answer options.

6. Using the random shuffle, randomize the order of the list of answers.

7. Create a string of the answers

8. Present the question and the options for answer to the player within an input.

9. Check the response from the player to see if they selected the correct answer. Apply the score

10. Provide feedback once all the questions are shown

11. Invoke the function to start the game

```python
import json
import random

file = open('data.json','r')
json = json.loads(file.read())

def quiz(questions):
    score = 0
    counter = 0
    for question in questions:
        counter += 1
        answers = question['answers']
        answers.append(question['correct'])
        correct = question['correct']
        random.shuffle(answers)
        opts = ' - '.join(answers)
        res =
input(question['question']+'\n'+opts+'? ')
        if res.lower() == correct.lower():
            print('Yes Correct')
            score += 1
        else:
            print(f'Wrong was {correct}')
    print(f'Game over! You scored {score}
out of {counter}')
quiz(json)


[{
    "question": "What color is an apple"
    , "answers": ["Blue",  "Purple"]
    , "correct": "Red"
}
  , {
```

```
      "question": "What color is Grass"
      , "answers": ["Blue", "Red", "Purple"]
      , "correct": "Green"
   }
    , {
      "question": "Is the Sky Blue"
      , "answers": [ "False"]
      , "correct": "True"
   }
   ]
```

Output result :
What color is an apple
Purple - Blue - Red? purple
Wrong was Red
What color is Grass
Green - Purple - Blue - Red? green
Yes Correct
Is the Sky Blue
False - True? true
Yes Correct
Game over! You scored 2 out of 3

This Python code is a quiz game that reads quiz questions and answers from a JSON file named 'data.json'. Here's an explanation of how the code works:

1. Import the json and random modules: The code begins by importing the json module for working with JSON data and the random module for shuffling answer options.

2. Open and Read the JSON File: It opens the 'data.json' file in read mode using open('data.json', 'r') and assigns the file object to the file variable.

3. Parse JSON Data: The code reads the contents of the file using the file.read() method and parses the JSON data into a Python list, which is stored in the json variable.

4. Define the Quiz Function: The quiz function is defined to take a list of quiz questions as its parameter.

5. Initialize Score and Counter: Inside the quiz function, two variables, score and counter, are initialized to keep track of the player's score and the number of questions answered.

6. Iterate Through Questions: The code then iterates through each question in the questions list.

o answers is a list containing answer options for the current question.

o correct stores the correct answer for the question.

o The correct answer is appended to the answers list.

o The answer options are shuffled randomly to change their order.

o The answer options are presented to the player, and their input is stored in the res variable.

7. Check Answer: The player's response is compared with the correct answer (ignoring case), and if it matches, a message saying "Yes Correct" is printed. Otherwise, the correct answer is displayed.

8. Score Calculation: The player's score is updated based on correct answers.

9. Game Over Message: After all questions have been answered, a "Game over!" message is printed, along with the player's final score and the total number of questions answered.

10. Calling the quiz Function: The quiz function is called with the parsed JSON data as its argument, allowing the player to play the quiz.

The provided JSON data represents a list of quiz questions, each with a question, answer options, and the correct answer. The player is presented with these questions, and their score is calculated based on correct answers.

Example JSON data (questions and answers) is provided as a sample at the end of the code to illustrate how the JSON structure should be formatted for the quiz.

Exercise Scrambled word guess

This exercise contains a number of the features that were presented in the previous exercises. There is a word list that will scramble the letters of the word asking the player to guess the correct word. Three guesses per word.

1. Import the random module

2. Create a list of words to use

3. Create a function named maker() that will shuffle the order of the letters in a string

4. Create a main game play function. Shuffle the order of the words in the list.
5. Let the player know how many words will be presented
6. Set a counter for the guesses and total number for the guesses guessed.
7. Loop through all the items in the words list.
8. Increment the counter by 1, set the guess value to blank. Set Up an inplay boolean value and set a variable to track the current number of guesses in the round.
9. Create a loop that will allow for 3 guesses per word, create the input question about the word.
10. Provide feedback to the player each word round.
11. Once the game is over provide the full scoring from the game play.

```python
import random
animals =
['cat','dog','snake','duck','bear','frog']

def maker(p):
 temp = list(p)
 random.shuffle(temp)
 return ''.join(temp)

def gameplay():
    random.shuffle(animals)
    ques = len(animals)
    print(f'There are a total of {ques}')
    counter = 0
```

```
    total = 0
    for animal in animals:
        counter += 1
        guess = ''
        inPlay = False
        cur = 0
        while guess != animal and
not(inPlay):
            if cur < 3:
                word = maker(animal)
                total += 1
                cur += 1
                guess = input(f'Which animal
is this {word}? ')
            else:
                inPlay = True
        if inPlay:
            print(f'Took too many guesses it
was {animal}')
        else:
            print(f'{animal} is correct you
are at {total} guesses and on the {counter}
animal')
    print(f'Game Over it took {total}
guesses to get all the values of {ques}
scrambled words. ')

gameplay()
```

Output result :
There are a total of 6
Which animal is this ogd? dog
dog is correct you are at 1 guesses and on the 1 animal
Which animal is this act? cat
cat is correct you are at 2 guesses and on the 2 animal
Which animal is this brea? bear

bear is correct you are at 3 guesses and on the 3 animal
Which animal is this ofgr? f
Which animal is this ogfr? d
Which animal is this fgro? frog
frog is correct you are at 6 guesses and on the 4 animal
Which animal is this kdcu? s
Which animal is this duck? a
Which animal is this kudc? s
Took too many guesses it was duck
Which animal is this asnke? s
Which animal is this nkaes? d
Which animal is this skane? d
Took too many guesses it was snake
Game Over it took 12 guesses to get all the values of 6
scrambled words.

This Python code is a word guessing game where the
player needs to unscramble words representing animal
names. Here's an explanation of how the code works:

1. Import the random module: The code begins by importing
   the random module for shuffling the list of animal names
   and for generating random words to scramble.

2. Define the maker Function: The maker function takes a
   string p, shuffles its characters, and returns the shuffled
   string. It is used to generate scrambled versions of animal
   names.

3. Define the gameplay Function: This function is the core of
   the word guessing game.

- It shuffles the list of animal names randomly using random.shuffle(animals) to change the order in which animals are presented to the player.
- It calculates the total number of questions (animal names) in the ques variable.
- It initializes counter to keep track of the current question number and total to keep track of the total number of guesses.
- It enters a loop that iterates through each animal name in the shuffled list.
- For each animal name, it sets guess to an empty string, inPlay to False, and cur to 0. These variables are used to track the player's progress in guessing the animal name.
- Inside a nested loop, it allows the player to guess the unscrambled animal name. If the player guesses incorrectly, they can try up to three times (controlled by the cur variable).
- If the player correctly guesses the animal name, it prints a message indicating success, the total number of guesses so far (total), and the current question number (counter).
- If the player takes more than three guesses (cur >= 3), the game sets inPlay to True and prints a message indicating that the player took too many guesses and reveals the correct animal name.

- After finishing all questions, it prints a "Game Over" message with the total number of guesses made to complete the game.

4. Calling the gameplay Function: The gameplay function is called to start the word guessing game.

In this game, the player is presented with scrambled animal names and must unscramble them to identify the correct animal. If the player takes more than three guesses for a single word, the game moves on to the next word, and the player is informed that they guessed incorrectly. The game continues until all animal names have been guessed or until the player decides to quit.

The player's performance is tracked in terms of the total number of guesses required to unscramble all the animal names.

In this chapter, we explored the fascinating world of Python programming through the lens of interactive word games and challenges. We began by leveraging Python's versatility and randomization capabilities to create engaging word-related games, including word unscrambling and word guessing. Through these examples, we not only had fun but also learned valuable Python programming concepts and techniques.

We discovered how to work with essential Python modules such as random, json, and datetime, which enriched our games with dynamic content, real-time clock interactions, and randomization. We also delved into the use of functions and loops to create interactive gameplay and manage game logic efficiently.

Throughout our journey, we encountered various Python data structures like lists, dictionaries, and modules, and we harnessed their power to build engaging and interactive experiences. From shuffling animal names to generating randomized passwords, we learned how to apply Python's core features creatively.

By exploring these Python coding examples, we've gained hands-on experience and a deeper understanding of Python's capabilities. We've unlocked the potential to develop a wide range of interactive applications, from educational games to utility scripts. As we continue our Python journey, the possibilities are endless, and we're well-equipped to tackle more complex challenges and projects. So, let's embrace the world of Python programming, armed with the knowledge and skills we've acquired in this chapter, and look forward to even more exciting adventures in coding.